PRACT[illegible]
WELDING
PROJECTS

25 INNOVATIVE METAL-WORK PROJECTS FOR HOBBY WELDERS

BY KAREN RUTH

APPLE

First published in the UK in 2006 by
Apple Press
Sheridan House
114 Western Road
Hove
East Sussex BN3 1DD
www.apple-press.com

ISBN-10: 1 84543 167 7
ISBN-13: 978 1 84543 167 9

Created and produced by
Creative Publishing international, Inc.
18705 Lake Drive East
Chanhassen, Minnesota 55317
USA
www.creativepub.com

Printed in China
10 9 8 7 6 5 4 3 2 1

Visit the following web sites for more information about the products used in this book:

ARCHITECTURAL IRON DESIGNS
www.archirondesign.com

CHANDELIERPARTS.COM
www.chandelierparts.com

DECORATIVE IRON
www.decorativeiron.com

HOOKER GLASS MIRROR & BEVELING CORP
www.miror.com

M-BOSS INC.
www.mbossinc.com

MAIN STREET SUPPLY
www.mainstsupply.com

METALS DEPOT
www.metalsdepot.com

NATIONAL ORNAMENTAL & MISCELLANEOUS METALS ASSOCIATION (NOMMA)
www.nomma.org

NORTON METALS
www.nortonmetals.com

SILENT SOURCE
www.silentsource.com

SMALL PARTS, INC.
www.smallparts.com

SMITH & HAWKEN
www.smithandhawken.com

TRIPLE-S STEEL SUPPLY CO.
www.sss-steel.com

WAGNER RAILING SYSTEMS
AND COMPONENTS
J.G. BRAUN COMPANY
www.rbwagner.com
www.jgbraun.com

CONTENTS

INTRODUCTION

Walk into any design or garden centre and you will see dozens of welded metal furnishings, from small candleholders to large gazebos. The price tags may give you sticker shock, but most of these items are surprisingly easy to make. Unlike working with wood, with its complicated joinery, working with mild steel is much easier. While it takes years to become a proficient industrial welder, in a highly skilled field, it takes only hours to learn to weld decorative projects.

The project designs in this book are similar to those you may see at a design center—folding screens, nesting tables, incidental tables, and lamps—and many you would see at a garden centre—arched arbors, gates, and gazebos. With twenty-five distinctly different projects, you are sure to find something you will enjoy making and love having on display. The projects range from simplistic—requiring a few cuts with a hacksaw, a few bends around piping, and a few welds—to more challenging—requiring flame or plasma cutting and extensive welding.

Each project includes a full-color photograph of the finished project, a technical exploded-view illustration of the project, a complete cutting and materials list, and step-by-step directions. Photographs of selected steps further illustrate the techniques used. A list of internet sites is provided on page 2 to help you locate and order the decorative materials used in the projects.

This book does not teach welding techniques. It is recommended that you take an introductory welding class before attempting these projects.

Practical Welding Projects is an excellent resource for any hobby welder. Use the projects as they appear, or modify them to suit your particular space and design needs. You won't be disappointed with how great the finished projects look in your home—or with the oohs and aahs of recipients when you give them as gifts.

HELPFUL NOTE: Many parts in this book are not premade, such as hooks, spirals, and circles. These parts are "blanks" (pieces that must be formed or created with the materials listed). The steps to create the parts are included in the project instructions.

NOTICE TO READERS:

Welding is a dangerous activity. Failure to follow safety procedures may result in serious injury or death. This book provides useful instructions, but we cannot anticipate all of your working conditions or the characteristics of your materials and tools. For safety, you should use caution, care, and good judgment when following the procedures described in this book. Consider your own skill level and the instructions and safety precautions associated with the various tools and materials shown. The publisher cannot assume responsibility for any damage to property or injury to persons as a result of misuse of the information provided.

Metal Shapes & Sizes

Mild steel (and most other metals) comes in a variety of shapes, sizes, and thicknesses. Metal thickness may be given as a fraction of an inch, a decimal, or a gauge (see chart, opposite page).

RECTANGULAR TUBE (A) AND SQUARE TUBE (B) are used for structural framing, trailers, and furniture. Dimensions for rectangular and square tubing are given as width × height × wall thickness × length.

RAIL CAP (C) is used for making handrails. Rail cap dimensions are the overall width and the widths of the channels on the underside.

CHANNEL (D) is often used for making handrails. Very large channel is used for truck bodies. The legs, or *flanges*, make it stronger than flat bars. Dimensions for channel are given as flange thickness × flange height × channel (outside) height × length.

ROUND TUBE (E) is not the same as pipe. Round tube is used for structures, and pipe is used for carrying liquids or gases. Dimensions for round tube are given as outside diameter (O.D.) × wall thickness × length. Pipe dimensions are nominal, that is, in name only. They are given as nominal inside diameter (I.D.) × length.

T-BAR (F) dimensions are given as width × height × thickness of flanges × length.

ANGLE OR ANGLE IRON (G) has many structural and decorative uses. Dimensions for angle iron are flange thickness × flange width × flange height × length.

SQUARE BAR (H), ROUND BAR (I), AND HEXAGONAL OR HEX BAR (J) dimensions are given as width or outside diameter × length.

FLAT BAR OR STRAP (NOT PICTURED) is available in many sizes. Dimensions are given as thickness × width × length.

SHEET METAL (NOT PICTURED) is 3⁄16" or less in thickness and is often referred to by gauge. Plate metal is more than 3⁄16" thick and is referred to by fractions or inches.

Purchasing Metal

Finding a metal supplier can be a challenging task. The materials that are readily available may not be the sizes and shapes needed for a project and may be expensive. Metal dealerships may not be friendly to small accounts. Because steel is so heavy, Internet or catalogue shopping carries prohibitive shipping costs. With some searching, however, most necessary materials can be found.

Metal is generally priced by weight, unless you are purchasing it at a retail store. The price for small pieces of mild steel at a home centre or hardware store work out to be as much as $3 to $5 per pound. The price per pound for small orders at a steel dealership may be in the range of $1. Large orders or repeat orders may be priced as low as 50 cents per pound. Many metal suppliers have an odds and ends bin or rack where pieces may be as low as 10 cents per pound. Specialty metals such as stainless steel and aluminum start at $2 to $3 per pound.

Smaller sizes and shapes of mild steel and aluminum are available at home improvement and hardware stores in three-, four-, and six-foot lengths. Welding supply stores often have a selection of ten- and twelve-foot lengths of the commonly used sizes. Steel dealers have most common sizes in stock and will order other sizes for you. Most mild steel shapes and sizes come in twenty-foot lengths, and many steel dealers will make one free courtesy cut per piece. You might want to have the metal delivered, depending on the amount of material you are purchasing.

Some steel dealers are distributors for decorative metal products, but many specialty items such as wrought iron railing materials, decorative items, and weldable hardware are only available by catalogue. A number of catalogue supply houses sell to the public and have varied selections and reasonable prices.

Inch Equivalent for Gauge Thickness

GAUGE	INCHES
24	0.020
22	0.026
20	0.032
18	0.043
16	0.054
14	0.069
12	0.098
11	0.113
10	0.128

Metal less than 1/8" thick is often referred to by gauge. For reference, the decimal equivalent of 1/8" is 0.125.

Sheet metal is available as pierced or expanded. Wall plates, hooks, rings, balls, bushings, candle cups, drip plates, and stamped or cast items are available in a wide variety of shapes, sizes, and metals.

Cutting Metal

For some projects, cutting the metal is the most difficult step. A variety of tools exist for cutting metal, but the thicker and larger the stock, the fewer your choices. If you want to build muscle, a hacksaw is great for tubes, rods, and bars, but a large project will soon have you wishing for some more powerful cutters. Cutting thin-gauge sheet metal can be done with sheet metal snips, but thicker gauges and plate require shears or cutting torches. You can spend a couple hundred pounds or a couple thousand pounds on power metal cutting tools. Here are some of your options.

SAFETY

- Welding helmet with #10 to #14 filter
- Long pants, long sleeved shirt, and hat
- Leather gloves
- Leather boots or shoes
- Ventilation

A horizontal metal cutting bandsaw is a bench-mounted bandsaw with clamps, to hold work pieces, and an automatic "shut off" feature that turns off the saw when the cut is completed. The most common cutting capacity is 4" × 6", which can cut through a rectangular piece of that dimension or a $4\frac{1}{2}$" round. A portable metal-cutting bandsaw is slightly less expensive than the bench version and obviously more portable. The most common size cuts 4" stock. It is more difficult to create accurate cuts with the portable bandsaw, but the portability makes the machine more versatile in a do-it-yourself shop. A distinct advantage of the bandsaws is the very small kerf (less than $\frac{1}{16}$").

Bimetal saw blades are the best for cutting metal, whether you are using them in your hacksaw or bandsaw. Make the blades in your hacksaw and portable bandsaw last longer by not forcing the cut, but allowing the saw to cut slowly and steadily. Excess pressure simply wears the blades out before their time.

Power tools for a welding shop include: A. reciprocating saw, B. chop saw, C. portable band saw, D. angle grinder.

Metal-cutting chop saws, cut-off machines, and angle grinders use abrasive wheels for cutting. These produce a great deal of heat and metal dust, and cut pieces typically have burred edges. Metal-cutting circular saws with carbide blades produce cleaner cuts with less heat. They are also faster than chop saws. Both of these types of saws have larger kerfs (at least $\frac{3}{32}$") than the bandsaw. A portable steel saw looks and operates like a standard circular saw, but is capable of cutting up to $\frac{1}{4}$" sheet metal, as well as cutting tube and rod. Reciprocating saws can also be used for cutting rod and tube.

Manual or hydraulic metal shears and punches in small sizes suitable for home shops are relatively inexpensive. They are limited to thin-gauge materials, usually less than 16 gauge. And, the heavier material capacity, the more expensive the machine.

Manual snips are sufficient for cutting curves in sheet metal less than 18 gauge. Power nibblers make quick work of curves, but are commonly available for 18-gauge (or less) thicknesses. An oxyacetylene cutting torch is a moderately priced option for cutting sheet metal. Its advantages are: it requires no power source, it cuts up to 12" thicknesses, and it is extremely portable. The disadvantages are: it has an increased hazard of fuel tanks, it is costly to rent the fuel tanks, and it takes a considerable amount of time to learn how to make clean cuts. If you have the money to spend and want to cut a lot of sheet metal in intricate patterns, the best tool is a plasma cutter. The small, portable models easily cut a 1/8" sheet while running off standard household power. They are simple to use and require the same safety gear as wire-feed welders. Plasma cutters can cut any material that conducts electricity; they are especially good at cutting expanded and pierced sheet metal. However, they do require a separate air compressor.

Drilling metal is fairly easy with a handheld drill or drill press.

Bending jigs can be made from any rigid circular item. An engine flywheel, toilet flange, and various pipe sizes are shown here.

Use a vise-style pliers to hold the metal to the jig. Wrap the metal around the jig in a smooth motion.

Use a scroll bender to bend decorative scrolls.

Shaping Metal

There are a number of ways to bend and shape mild steel. Brakes, for creating angles in sheet metal, and ring rollers and scroll benders to create circles and scrolls are readily available for the home crafter. Unfortunately, the higher the capacity of these bending tools, the higher the price.

You can make simple bending jigs from any round, rigid, strong form, such as pipe and salvaged flywheels, pulley wheels, or wheel rims. Using these jigs, it is fairly easy to bend round rod up to 1/4" and flat bars up to 1/8" into complex shapes. A bench vise is handy for making acute bends. Tubing, rail cap, and channel can be bent with a heavy-duty, electrical conduit bender. With practice and patience, you can create well-formed circles by making incremental bends with the conduit bender.

Thicker materials are bent more easily if you have a long end for applying pressure; it is better to cut pieces to length after bending. Sliding a pipe over a short end will increase your leverage. When shaping metal into sharp bends, take into account the length needed for the radius of the bend. Cold-formed metal springs back somewhat, so it may take trial and error to find which size jig makes the bend size you desire.

Cleaning Metal

A successful weld begins with a well-prepared piece of metal. The cleaner the pieces to be welded, the better the weld quality and appearance. Steel is not available in a pre-cleaned state, so you will need to clean all project parts by removing oil, mill scale, dirt, and rust. Although this can be a tedious step, a well-cleaned project lasts many years and you soon forget the time spent conscientiously cleaning every piece.

Use denatured alcohol to clean dirt and oil from project parts. Wear rubber gloves to protect your hands.

For any project that will be painted, it is important to thoroughly clean the entire part. For objects that will be allowed to rust gracefully outdoors, thoroughly clean the joint areas and allow the weather to clean the remainder.

The first step in cleaning is to wipe down the part with denatured alcohol, acetone, or a commercial degreaser to remove oil and dirt. The alcohol works best as it has little odor, unlike the degreaser, and it won't dissolve plastics, like the acetone. Both acetone and degreasers tend to leave a residue that may diminish the quality of the final finish.

Once the grease, oil, and dirt have been removed from the surface, the mill scale (often found on mild steel) must be removed. Mill scale is a dark gray, flaky oxide layer that forms on the steel as it cools. Cold rolled steel often has a thinner layer of scale than hot rolled steel, but even the thin layer needs to be removed before welding and finishing. Manufacturers use a pickling bath to remove scale; except for very small projects, it is unlikely that a home do-it-yourselfer would want to work with the hot acid bath needed for pickling. The remaining options are wire brushing, grinding, sanding, or sandblasting.

Cleaning the mill scale off mild steel is an important step. A bench-mounted power wire brush works well on small pieces. Wire brushing the entire project prior to finishing is critical for good paint adhesion.

A bench-mounted power wire brush is perfect for cleaning the ends of parts. Unfortunately, it is not suitable for cleaning the remaining surfaces. For this you will need an angle grinder outfitted with a wire brush cup or flap sander. A drill or rotary tool with a wire brush wheel, wire brush cup, or flap sander also works well. When working with power wire brushes it is crucial you wear appropriate protective gear. A full face mask and long sleeves protects your eyes and arms from wire fragments that are thrown from the brush. Heavy leather gloves will protect your fingertips from getting skinned. These tools operate at very high speeds and can quickly do serious damage to eyes and skin.

Once the metal has been cleaned and de-scaled, it is important that you complete the project in a timely manner so that it does not start to rust.

FINISHING METAL

A nice finish adds to the beauty of your welded project. Unless you intend to let your project fully rust, even bare metal needs some type of coating. Applying a paint coating is best done by spraying, not brushing.

If you look closely at most welded furniture or garden accessories you'll see that these items typically have rough welds and spatter. With your own projects, especially indoor projects, taking the time to grind down welds and grind off spatter is time well spent. A nicely ground, good weld looks like a continuous, solid piece of metal. This is especially important for glossy finishes, as a smooth, shiny paint job will highlight even the tiniest imperfections.

A primer coat is recommended underneath all but bare metal coatings. If deeply rusted areas cannot be cleaned to bare metal, use a rusty metal primer or, even better, a rust converter on the rusted area. Carefully read product labels, as some converters require oil-based top coats and other specific finishes.

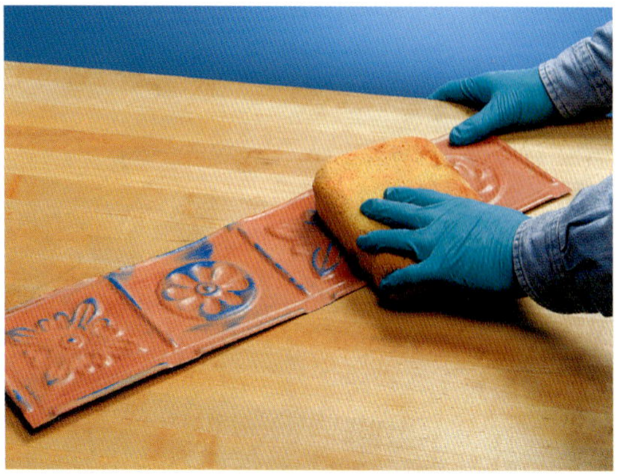

One method for creating an antique finish is to apply two wet top coats of different colors to a dry base coat of a third color. Before the top coats dry, wipe the top coats off in selected areas with a wet sponge.

A wide variety of spray-on finishes is available. With one application you can create a hammered texture or a granite look (Rustoleum® Stone Creations, for example). Crackle and antiquing looks are also available. Verdigris finishes involve more steps and time, but create a unique look that is very impressive. Railing and gate suppliers carry a variety of primers, paints, dyes, and patinas to give your project a one-of-a-kind look.

Bare metal can be sanded, ground, or heated to create intriguing looks. To prevent rust, coat bare metal with a clear coat or a metal polish.

There are a number of ways to create an antique or aged painted finish. One is to paint the surface with three or four layers of different paint colours, allowing each layer to dry thoroughly between coats. When the final coat is dry, sand off corners and high spots to reveal the paint layers. Another method is to apply one colour layer and allow it to dry completely. Then apply a second layer and third layer without allowing drying time. Use a damp sponge to wipe off layers at corners and high spots (see photo). To create a crackly, "alligatored" paint look, purchase crackle base and crackle top coat, either as a spray paint or brush on paint. Apply the two coats as directed to create the crackle effect (see samples photo).

There are many possibilities for finishing metal. Pictured here, from left to right: brush-on crackle finish, spray painted stone, spray painted hammered metal, and a swirl pattern created with an angle grinder.

Swivel Mirror

Reflect your great taste with this sturdy, modern mirror. Its classic design creates a mirror built to last and will make a stunning first impression when displayed in your front entryway for years to come. The clean lines and black paint give this mirror a modern feel, but this can easily be altered by the finish treatment you choose. The adjustable mirror allows even the most petite guests to swivel it to the perfect height.

As described here, the inside frame is welded to the outside frame from the back, using numerous small welds. The joints between the inside frame pieces are welded from the front, and those welds are ground down. The final look is a frame within a frame, rather than a completely smooth single frame. If you prefer a solid frame, you may continuously weld the inside frame to the outside frame from the front and then grind the welds smooth.

MATERIALS

- 16-gauge 1 × 1" square tube (22 feet)
- ⅛ × ½" flat bar (11 feet)
- ½ × ½" square bar (7")
- 1½" × 5/16" hex bolts (2)
- ¼"–20 hex nuts (6)
- Levellers (4, Rockler #32498)
- ½ × 1" flat bar (6")
- Mirror (45⅞" × 17⅞")
- ¼" fiberboard (46" × 18")

Screw handle detail

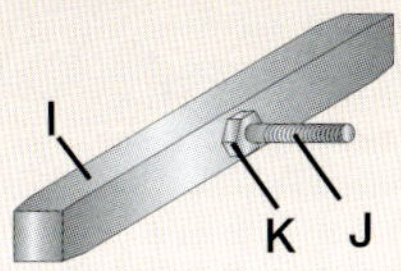

Frame detail

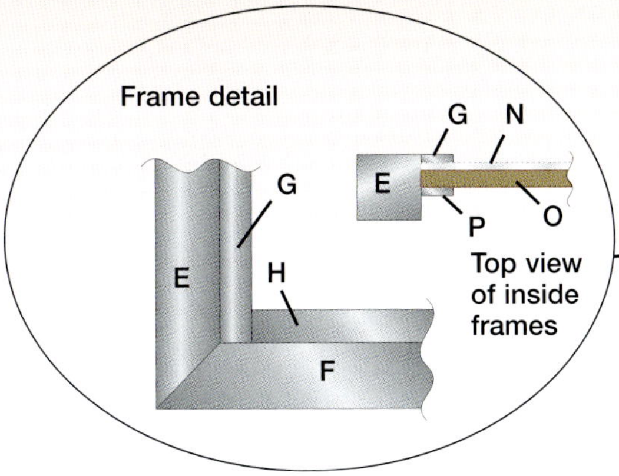

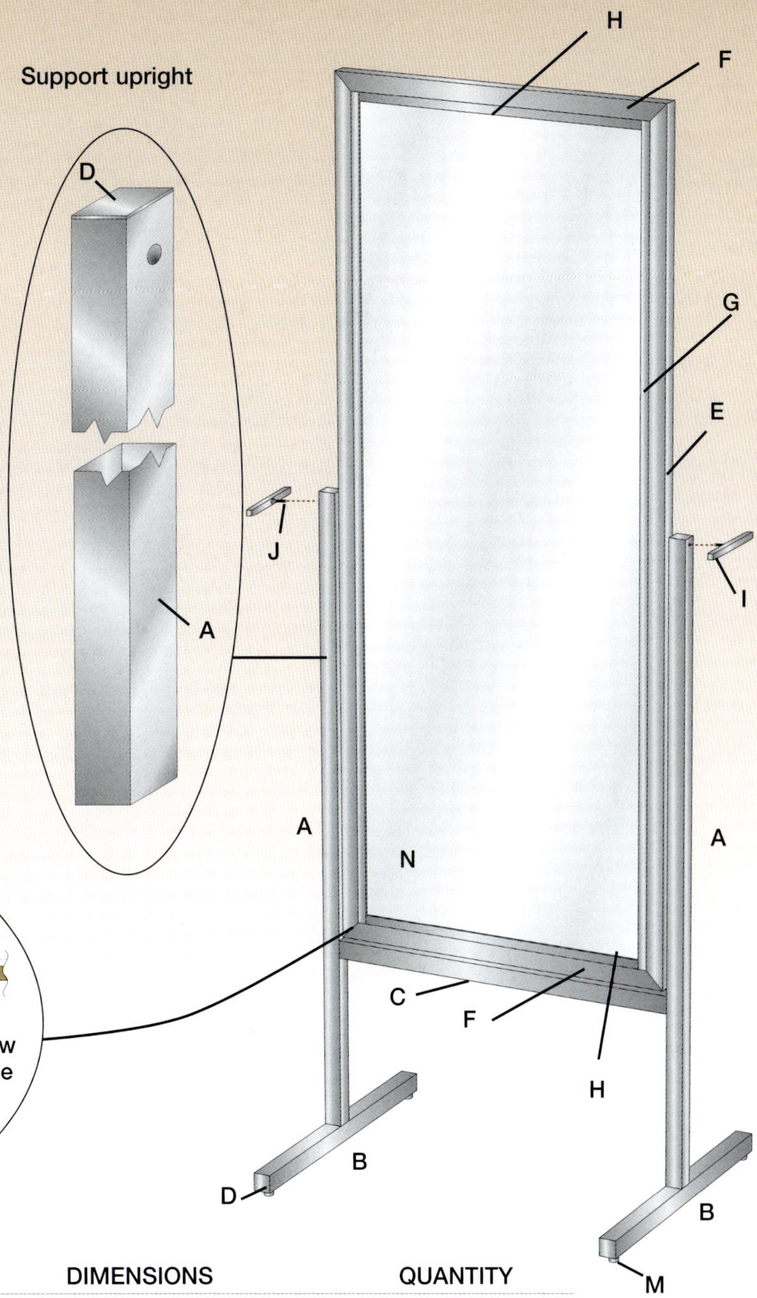

PART	NAME	DIMENSIONS	QUANTITY
A	Support uprights	16-gauge 1 × 1" square tube × 36"	2
B	Support bases	16-gauge 1 × 1" square tube × 18"	2
C	Crossbar	16-gauge 1 × 1" square tube × 18½"*	1
D	End caps	⅛ × 1" flat bar × 1"	6
E	Frame sides	16-gauge 1 × 1" square tube × 48"	2
F	Frame ends	16-gauge 1 × 1" square tube × 20"	2
G	Inside frame sides	⅛ × ½" flat bar × 46"	2
H	Inside frame ends	⅛ × ½" flat bar × 17"	2
I	Screw handles	½ × ½" square bar × 3½"	2
J	Handle bolts	1 ½" hex bolt	2
K	Handle nuts	¼"–20 hex nut	2
L	Leveller nuts (optional)	¼"–20 hex nut	4
M	Levellers (optional)		4
N	Mirror	45¾" × 17¾"*	1
O	Mirror backing	45⅞" × 17⅞"* fiberboard	1
P	Tabs	⅛ × ½" flat bar × ½"	8

* Approximate measurement, cut to fit.

How to Build a Swivel Mirror

Before welding, thoroughly clean all parts with denatured alcohol.

ASSEMBLE THE SUPPORTS

1. Cut the supports upright (A) and support base pieces (B) to length.
2. If using levelers, drill two 1 17⁄64" holes in one side of each loose piece, 2" from the ends. Drill through one wall only. Weld 1⁄4" hex nuts over the holes.
3. Centre an upright on a base at 90° and check for square. Weld into place and repeat with the second upright and base.
4. At 2" from the top outside of each upright, drill a 11⁄32" hole. Drill the hole through both walls of the tube.
5. Cut end caps (D) to size. Weld caps to the support upright and base ends (see photo, top right). The two supports are in the shape of a T, thus creating the need for six end caps.
6. Grind all welds smooth.

ASSEMBLE THE FRAME

1. Cut the frame sides (E) and frame ends (F) to size. Mitre the ends at 45°, or create a joint as shown in the Frame Detail (on page 13).
2. Drill a 11⁄32" hole at the outside midpoint of each side, through one wall, for the mirror pivot bolts.
3. Align a frame side and a frame end to make a 90° angle. Use a carpenter's square to check for square and clamp in place. Tack-weld the pieces together to form an L. Repeat with the other frame side and frame end.
4. Align the two Ls to form a rectangle. Use a carpenter's square to check for square. Clamp into place. Measure the diagonals of the rectangle to check for square. The diagonal measures should be equal; if not, adjust until they are. Tack-weld together and recheck for square.
5. Complete all the frame welds. Grind down each weld until flush.
6. Grind the zinc coating off the handle nuts (K). Centre the nuts over the holes and weld into place. Protect threads with anti-spatter gel (see photo, lower left).

ASSEMBLE THE INSIDE FRAME

1. Before cutting the inside frame sides (G) to length, measure the inside length of the assembled frame. Cut the inside frame sides to fit.
2. Place the assembled frame on a flat surface. Place the two inside frame sides in place against the two frame sides and tack-weld into place.
3. Measure between the inside frame sides and cut the inside frame ends (H) to length.
4. Place the inside frame ends in place against the frame ends and tack-weld into place.
5. Turn the frame unit over. The inside frame should be flush with the frame. If not, remove pieces and retack, as necessary.
6. Weld the inside frame to the frame from the back with small welds every 3" to 4". Weld the joints between the inside frame members from the front.
7. Grind down all the welds on the front so they are flush.

Tack-weld the end caps in place, then weld and grind the welds smooth.

Weld the nuts over the holes in the frame sides before assembling the frame. Use anti-splatter gel to protect the nut threads.

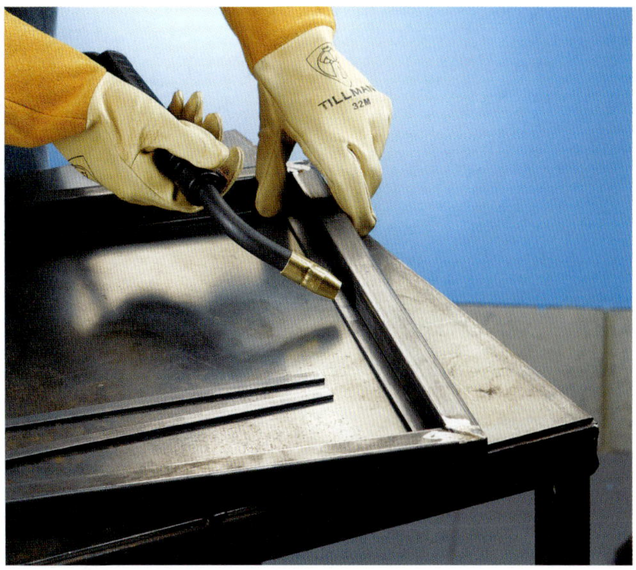

From the back, weld the inside frame to the frame. A small weld every 3" to 4" is sufficient.

Weld the bolts to the beveled screw handles. Use masking tape or anti-spatter gel to protect the threads.

MAKE THE HANDLES, AND APPLY FINISH

1. Cut the screw handles (I) to length. Bevel the ends.
2. Grind the zinc coating from the head of the handle bolt (J). Coat the bolt threads with anti-spatter gel or cover with masking tape. Weld the bolts to the centre of the bolt handles (see photo, above).
3. Assemble the frame and supports. With the bolts tightened enough to prevent the frame from moving, measure the distance between the support uprights, making sure the uprights are parallel during measurement. Cut the support crossbar (C) to this length.
4. Measure the distance between the frame and the uprights (it should be about ¼"). Mark the uprights below the frame at that same distance. The top of the crossbar will align with these marks so the spacing between the frame and uprights and crossbar is uniform.
5. Disassemble the frame and supports. Align the top of the crossbar with the marks on the uprights. (This is easiest with support bases hanging over the edge of the work surface.) Tack-weld the crossbar into place (see photo, opposite top). Use a carpenter's square to check that all angles between the crossbar and support uprights are 90°. Complete the welds and grind them smooth.
6. Grind all welds smooth and grind off any spatter. Wipe the parts down with denatured alcohol to remove grinding dust. Prime and paint. For a natural metal look, use a clear coat. Protect bolt and nut threads with tape during painting to prevent fouling. Don't forget to paint the handles.

Assemble the frame and uprights and mark the location for the crossbar. Remove the frame and weld the crossbar in place.

INSTALL THE MIRROR

1. Measure the inside of the completed frame to determine the exact mirror size to order. The mirror (N) should be ¼" shorter and ¼" narrower than the frame.
2. Cut the mirror backing (O) to size.
3. Apply small dots of silicone adhesive every 12" around the inside frame. Place the mirror into the frame.
4. Apply small dots of silicone adhesive to the back of the mirror. Place the backing against the mirror. Place the mirror assembly face down on a non-scratching surface.
5. Cut the tabs (P) to size and grind one end to a semi-circle.
6. Space the tabs at 6", 23", and 40" along the frame sides. Sand a small amount of paint off the frame at these points. Centre a tab along the frame top and bottom.
7. Firmly push the tabs against the mirror backing and frame sides. Weld into place (see photo, right).
8. Paint the tabs and the smooth side of the mirror backing to match the frame.
9. Install the levellers, if desired, and assemble the mirror. Position the mirror within the uprights, and thread the handle bolts through the support uprights and into the frame sides.

Install the mirror and back in the frame. Sand the finish from the frame and weld the tabs per Step 6.

Square Bar Coat Hanger

This chic coat hanger has a modern artistic flair due to the unique circular patterns. But the basic design has unlimited potential. You can customise this rack for any part of your life—the front entryway, the garage, the gardening shed, and the cabin may all have different styles. Simply replace the spirals with a punched tin pattern, decorative frieze, or dragonfly, moose, or bear stampings. The rack is sized to mount on studs spaced 16 inches apart. If you like the spirals but want more contrast, use copper or brass 14-gauge wire and leave the entire piece unpainted—but be sure to braze the spirals into place, instead of welding them.

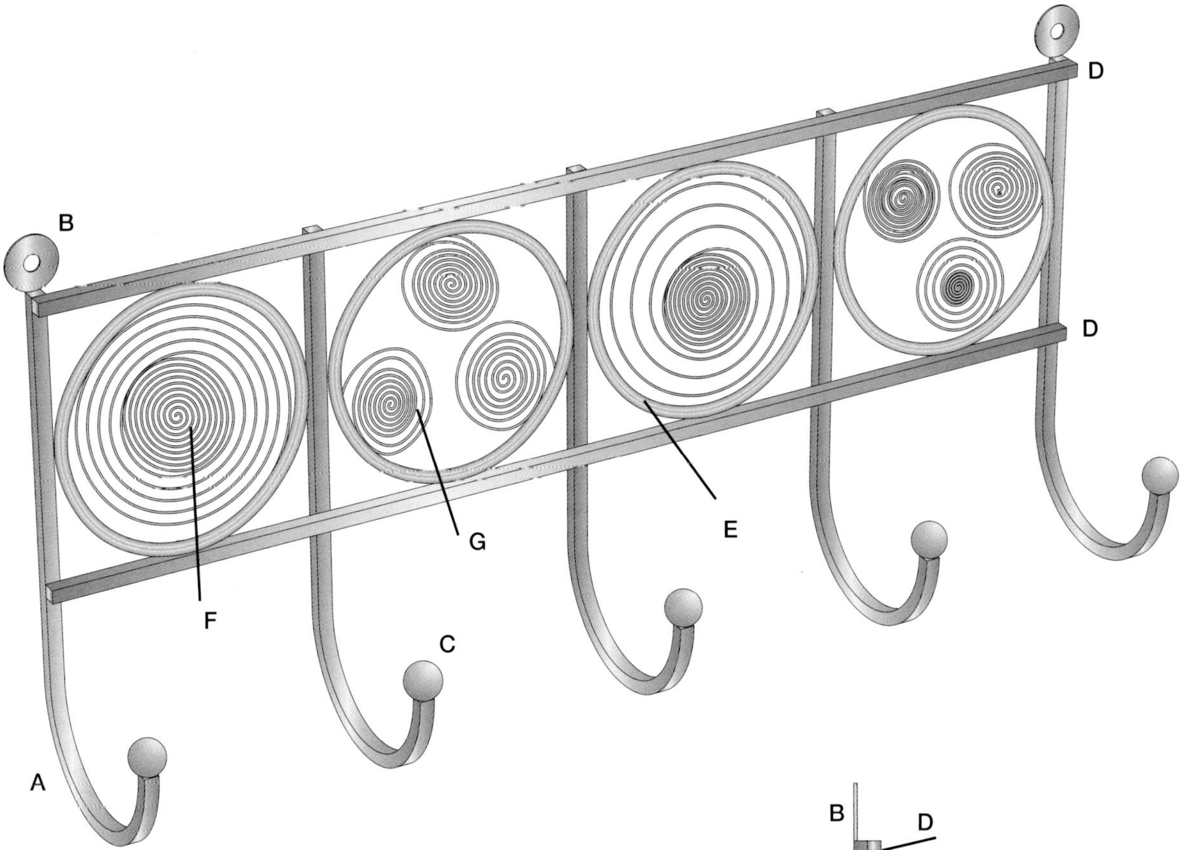

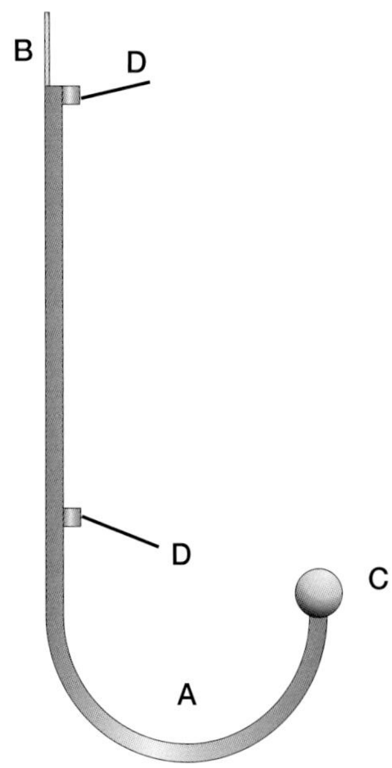

MATERIALS

- $^3/_{16}$" square bar (8 feet)
- $^1/_8$" square rod (8 feet)
- $^1/_2$" balls (5, Decorative Iron #JG8851)
- $^3/_4$" washers (2)
- 18-gauge annealed stove pipe wire (25 feet)

PART	NAME	DIMENSIONS	QUANTITY
A	Hooks	$^3/_{16}$" square bar × 11$^1/_2$"	5
B	Mounting washers	$^3/_4$"	2
C	Balls	$^1/_2$"	5
D	Crossbars	$^3/_{16}$" square bar × 16"	2
E	Circles	$^1/_8$" square rod × 24"	4
F	Mini-spirals	18-gauge wire	6
G	Spirals	18-gauge wire	2

How to Build a Square Bar Coat Hanger

Before welding, thoroughly clean all parts with denatured alcohol.

MAKE THE HOOKS AND FRAME

1. Cut the hooks (A) to length.
2. Clamp one end of each hook to a 2"-diameter pipe with a vise-style pliers. Bend the bar a ½ turn around the pipe to create each hook.
3. Weld each of the two mounting washers (B) to the top of two separate hooks (see photo, below). Weld a ball (C) to the end of all hooks.
4. Cut the crossbars (D) to length. Mark the crossbars at 4", 8", and 12".
5. Align the two hooks that have the mounting washers flush with the crossbar ends. Tack-weld in place. Place the second crossbar 4" from the top crossbar and tack-weld in place. Check that the angle between the crossbars and hooks is 90° and finish the welds.
6. Centre a hook under the two crossbars at the 12" mark, lining the top of the hook flush with the top crossbar. Check that the angle between the hook and crossbars is 90° and weld into place.
7. Weld the remaining two hooks to the crossbars at 4" and 8" (see photo, opposite left).

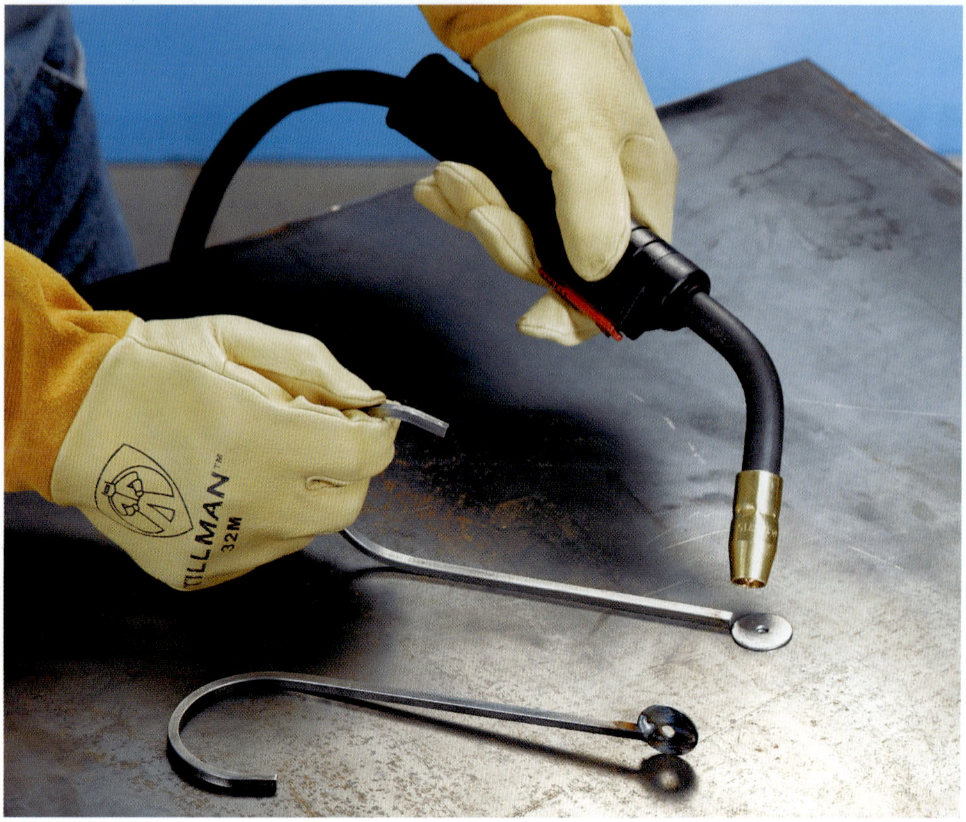

Weld the mounting washers to two of the hooks.

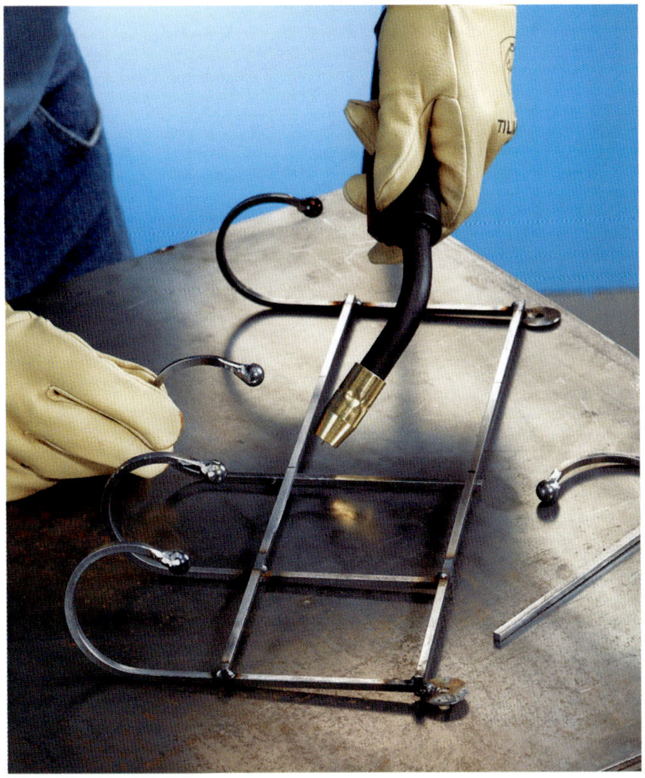

Weld the crossbars to the end hooks. Then weld the remaining hooks centred at 4", 8", and 12".

Begin a spiral by wrapping the wire around the tip of a needlenose pliers. Then grip the circle in the pliers and bend the wire until the desired size spiral is achieved.

MAKE THE CIRCLES AND SPIRALS

1. Cut the circles (E) to length.
2. Clamp one end of a circle blank to a 4" pipe, using a vise-style pliers. Bend the rod around the pipe 1½ turns to form a circle. Repeat to form the remaining circles.
3. Create the spirals (F) and mini-spirals (G) using a needlenose pliers. Wrap the wire around the end of the pliers to create a circle. Remove the circle from the pliers and grip it in the pliers. Wrap the wire around the circle until the desired size spiral has been formed (see photo, above right).

ASSEMBLE THE DECORATIVE FEATURES

1. Place a circle in the space between the first two hooks, starting either on the far left or far right end. Squeeze or expand the circle to fit into the space and cut off any extra length. Weld the circle ends together and weld the circle to the two hooks.
2. Repeat Step 2 with the remaining circles.
3. Arrange three mini-spirals inside the second and fourth circles. Weld them to each other and to the circle at contact points.
4. Place the large spirals between the remaining hooks and weld in place.
5. Wire brush or sandblast the coat hanger. Apply the desired finish.

Three-Panel Room Divider

Folding screens are versatile interior design pieces. Used as an accent behind furniture, as a room divider, or as a way to hide an unsightly outlet or wall blemish, this piece holds its own as a piece of art but is also practical furniture. In large spaces it provides a focus while also creating a seamless flow throughout the room. But don't limit this folding screen to indoor spaces. The all-metal version presented here could easily be incorporated into a garden as a trellis or fence panel.

This project includes two options. You can make a gathered fabric panel or a decorative metal panel. Or you could create both together. As constructed, this screen is moderately sized. Measure the area where the screen will reside and change the proportions accordingly.

Any number of decorative options can be used for the screen panels. Stained glass and pierced or expanded sheet metal are options not covered here, but they would be fabulous additions. If you spend some time with the catalogues of the decorative metal suppliers you will discover many leaf and flower stampings that could be used to create your own personalized pattern. Grapevines, oak leaves, and sunflowers are available in many different sizes; animal figures, sporting figures, and numbers and letters are available as well.

Note: If you don't care to cut out the leaves as listed in this project, use the small dapped leaf (#10392) by Architectural Iron Designs. It is slightly smaller than the leaves described in this project, but it is a similar pattern.

MATERIALS

- 16-gauge 3/4" round tube (49 feet)
- 16-gauge 1" round tube (2 feet)
- 1/4" round rod (8 feet)
- Fabric (5 yards)
- 16-gauge 1/2" round tube (28 feet)
- 1/8" round rod (14 feet)
- 22-gauge sheet metal (12 × 24")

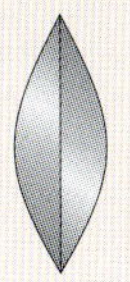

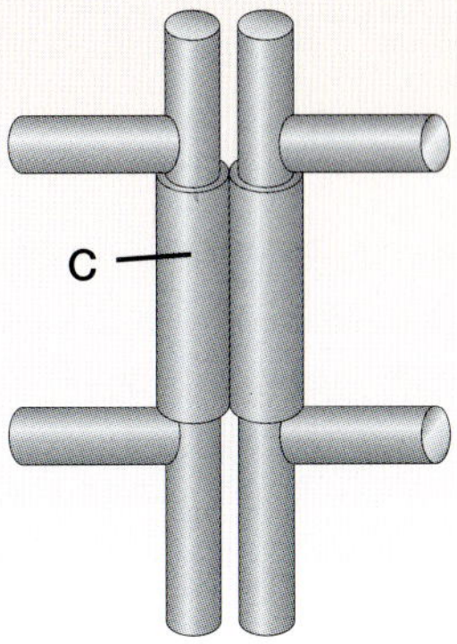

PART	NAME	DIMENSIONS	QUANTITY
A	Legs	16-gauge 3/4" round tube × 68"	6
B	Crossbars	16-gauge 3/4" round tube × 15"	12
C	Hinges	1/8 × 1" round tube × 3"	8
D	Fabric hanging rods (optional)	1/4" round rod × 15 1/2"	4
E	Fabric (optional)	60 × 30"	2
F	Verticals	16-gauge 1/2" round tube × 54 3/4"	6
G	Stems	1/8" round rod*	15
H	Leaves	22-gauge sheet metal × 4 × 1 1/2"*	45

* Approximate measurement, cut to fit.

How to Build a Three-Panel Room Divider

Before welding, thoroughly clean all parts with denatured alcohol.

MAKE THE FRAMES

1. Cut the legs and crossbars (A and B) to length.
2. Mark each leg at 6" in from each end.
3. Using a bench or angle grinder, grind the end of each crossbar to shape it to fit around the leg. Make sure the curves are oriented in the same direction at both ends (see photo, below).
4. Place two legs on a large work surface. Align the bottom of one crossbar and the top of another with the 6" marks. Tack-weld the crossbars in place. Check the frame for square and weld in place. Grind the welds smooth.
5. Repeat Step 4 for the remaining two panels.

ADD THE HINGES AND COMPLETE THE FRAMES

1. Cut the hinges (C) to length.
2. Slide the hinges over all four leg ends of one panel and the top and bottom leg ends of the one side of the other two panels.
3. Align the second set of crossbars above and below the hinges and tack-weld in place. Check for square and weld. Make certain you are not welding the hinges to the legs as you weld the crossbars.

OPTION 1: CREATE A FABRIC PANEL

The fabric panel is gathered. If you prefer a smooth look, decrease the fabric width to 15½".

Make the Hanging Rods

1. Cut the hanging rods (D) to length.
2. Mark points on the inside of each panel leg, ½" down from the inside top and bottom crossbars.
3. At the marked points, drill a 17/64" hole through the leg wall.
4. Insert one end of a hanging rod into a hole until it contacts the opposite wall. It should then be possible to insert the other end of the hanging rod into the hole on the opposite leg. If it is too long, grind it down until it fits.
5. Lay the three panels flat and parallel to each other, hinges touching. Weld each pair of hinges together (see photo, far right).
6. Grind down any rough welds and grind off spatter. Wipe down with denatured alcohol to remove grinding dust. Finish as desired.

Grind a semicircle in the crossbar ends to create a saddle to fit around the legs.

Make the Fabric Panel

1. Make a 1/4", flat-felled hem on the long sides of the fabric.
2. Drape the fabric over the top hanging rod so that equal amounts are extending past the top and bottom hanging rods.
3. Pin the fabric together around the rods.
4. Remove the rods and sew the rod pocket, turning the raw edge under.
5. Slide the fabric over the rods and reinstall the rods.

OPTION 2: CREATE A DECORATED PANEL

Make the Supports and Stems

1. Cut the verticals (F) to length.
2. Mark the interior crossbars at 5" and 10".
3. Centre the supports over the marks and tack-weld in place. Check for square and complete the welds. Grind the welds smooth.
4. Lay out the stems (G) in the desired pattern across the supports.

Make the Leaves

1. Cut the leaves (H) to desired size, using a tin snips or plasma cutter.
2. Place a leaf lengthwise in a bench vise and slightly bend it to form a crease down the centre.
3. Arrange the leaves in clusters of three. Weld the leaves together at the base (see photo, below left).
4. Place the leaf clusters on the stem ends and weld in place.
5. Lay out the three panels parallel to each other, hinges touching. Weld each pair of hinges together (see photo, below right).
6. Grind down any rough welds and grind off any spatter. Wipe down with denatured alcohol to remove grinding dust. Finish as desired.

Arrange the leaves in sets of three. Weld the points together, then weld the stem to the leaf sets.

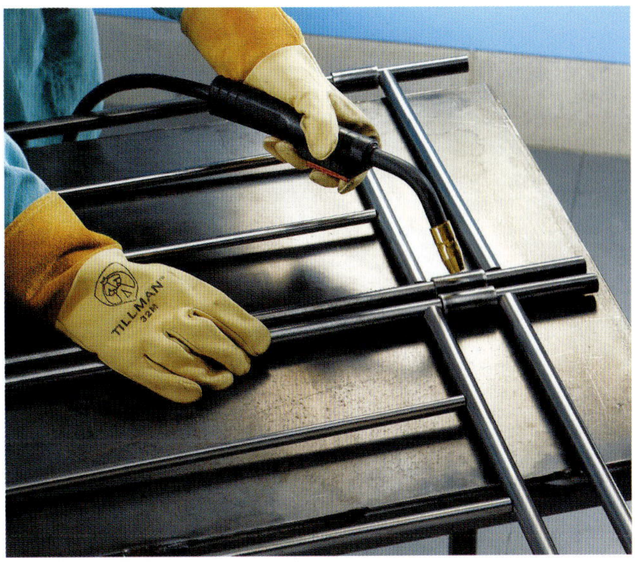

Align the hinge barrels and weld them together.

Tabletop Easel

Display your treasures with this simple easel. The design can be adjusted in size to display miniatures or serving platters by simply increasing or decreasing part sizes and support heights. For larger, floor-sized easels, increase the rod diameter as well; this allows the easel to support added weight. If the easel's purpose is to hold a showpiece but not steal too much of the attention, use antiquing finishes for a subtle yet elegant finish. For added pizzazz, try a verdigris or gold leaf finish (available at your local craft store). Add detail by incorporating small balls or florets on the supports.

PART	NAME	DIMENSIONS	QUANTITY
A	Legs	3⁄16" round rod × 15"	2
B	Rear leg	3⁄16" round rod × 14"	1
C	Hinge barrel	1⁄2" round tube × 3"	1
D	Hinge pin	3⁄8" round rod × 3 1⁄8"	1
E	Stop	3⁄16" round rod × 6"	1
F	Supports	3⁄16" round rod × 1"	2

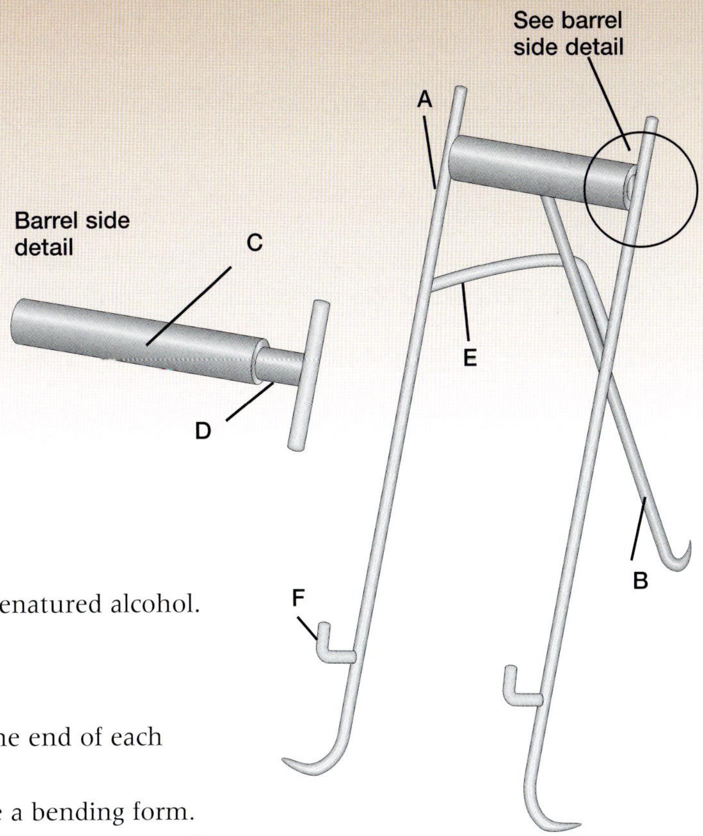

MATERIALS

- 3/16" round rod (52")
- 1/2" round tube (3")
- 3/8" round rod (3 1/8")

How to Build a Tabletop Easel

Before welding, thoroughly clean all parts with denatured alcohol.

MAKE THE LEGS

1. Cut the legs (A) and rear leg (B) to length.
2. Using a grinder, taper the last two inches of one end of each leg down to about 1/8".
3. Cut a 1/8" notch in a piece of 1/2" pipe to create a bending form.
4. Insert the tapered leg end into the notch and bend incrementally to form a curl. Then bend the leg part way around the outside of the pipe.
5. Repeat Step 4 for the other two legs. After bending, trim the front legs to be equal in length.

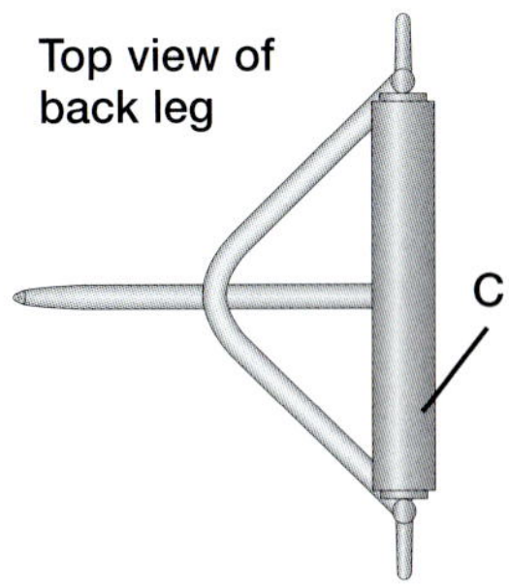

MAKE THE HINGE AND ATTACH THE LEGS

1. Cut the hinge barrel (C) and pin (D) to length.
2. Weld the back leg to the centre point of the hinge barrel, making sure the scroll is perpendicular to the barrel and curling up and away from the barrel.
3. Mark 1/2" down from the top of the front legs. On a flat surface, align the hinge pin with the mark on the right leg. Weld the pin to the leg (see photo, below).
4. Slide the barrel over the hinge pin. Swing the back leg up so the assembly can lie flat. Align the hinge pin with the mark on the left leg and weld the pin to the leg.

ATTACH THE STOP AND SUPPORTS

1. Cut the stop (E) to length. Clamp the midpoint to a 1/2" round tube and bend until the ends are three inches apart.
2. Lay the easel face down. Align the stop ends flush against the back of the two front pieces. If the stop is too high or too low, bend the front legs apart until they meet the stop. The stop should be slightly lower than the hinge, allowing the rear leg to support the easel. Hold the stop perpendicular to the front legs and weld in place.
3. Cut the supports to length and weld onto the two front legs, 2" up from the ends, and bend to 90°.
4. Grind down all welds. Wire brush or sandblast. Finish with your choice of finish.

Weld the back leg to the hinge barrel, then weld the hinge pin to one front leg.

PART	NAME	DIMENSIONS	QUANTITY
A	Vertical base	⅛ x 1½" flat bar x 30"	1
B	Horizontal bases	⅛ x 1½" flat bar x 10"	2
C	Vertical top	½" hammered bar x 29"	1
D	Horizontal tops	½" hammered bar x 9"	2
E	Rosette	2"	1
F	Scroll set	10 x 10"	1
G	Finials	5¼ x 2⅜"	4

Iron Cross

Rusted iron cross wall hangings evoke a sense of history. They create a distinctive air of mystery when hung over a fireplace or against exposed brickwork. Design centres and antique stores want hundreds of dollars for something that you can make for much less, so run wild with your imagination on this project and create a cross that personally resonates with you. The more ornate, the better. Search the catalogues from the suppliers for just the right touches—you'll find dozens of decorative pieces to make this project uniquely yours.

Rather than purchasing a 10- or 20-foot length of hammered or decorative bar—that's a lot of crosses—buy two 39" hammered railing pickets. To get a natural rust finish, thoroughly clean the completed cross with denatured alcohol, wet it down with salt water, and allow it to sit outside for a few months. You'll end up with a naturally beautiful rust.

Materials

- 1/8 × 1 1/2" flat bar (4 1/2 feet)
- 1/2" hammered bar (4 1/2 feet, Decorative Iron PM-013)
- 2" rosette (1, Decorative Iron LRD-65)
- Scroll set (1, Architectural Iron #55/9)
- Finials (4, Architectural Iron #81/3)

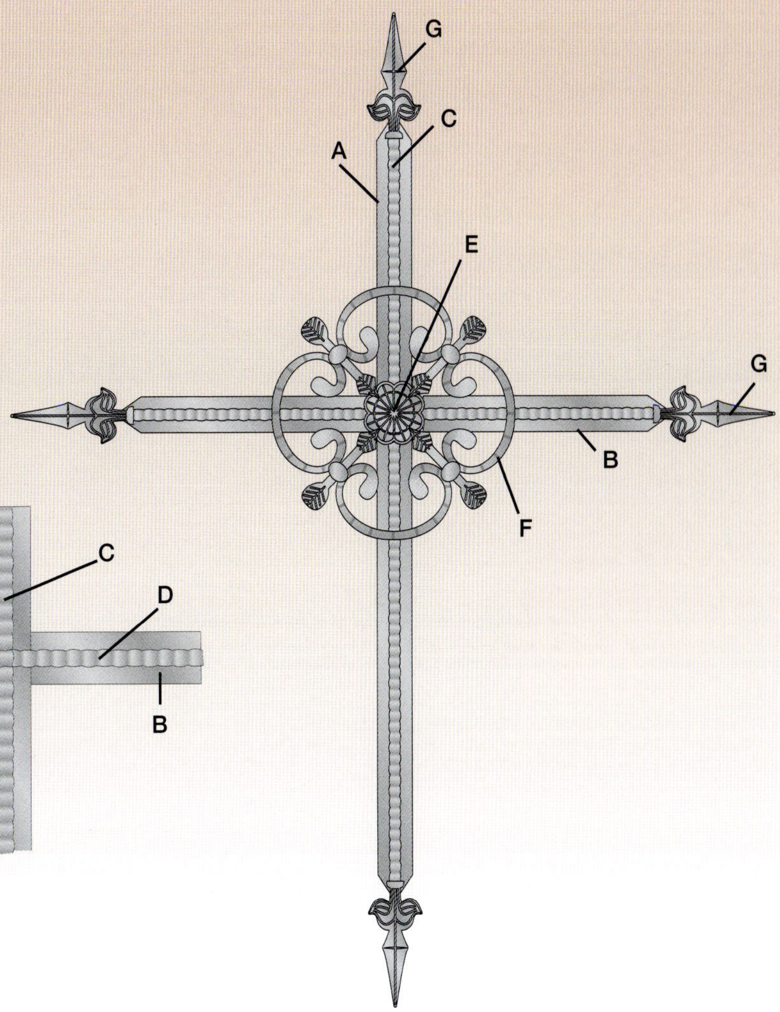

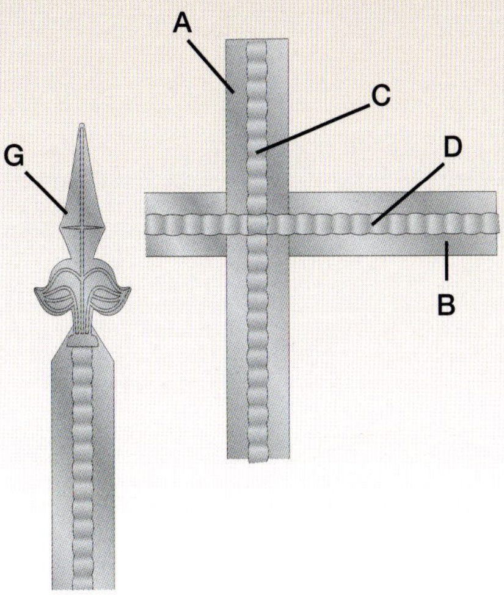

How to Build an Iron Cross

Before welding, thoroughly clean all parts with denatured alcohol.

MAKE THE BASE

1. Cut the base bars (A and B) to length.
2. Mark the centre point of each end of the vertical base and one end of each horizontal base. Mark the bars 1" in from the ends. Draw lines from the 1" mark to the centre point to create a point (see photo, below). Cut along the lines.
3. Mark the vertical base 11" from one end. Centre the two horizontal bases at this mark to form the cross. Check for square and weld in place. Grind the welds smooth.

MAKE THE TOP

1. Cut the vertical and horizontal tops (C and D) to length.
2. Centre the top vertical bar on the base. The points should extend ½" to ¾" beyond the bar ends. Weld the top bar to the base with 2 to 3 welds along each side (see photo, opposite top).
3. Centre the top horizontals on the base. They should touch the top vertical bar at the centre and end about an inch before the points. Weld in place.

ADD THE DECORATIVE ELEMENTS

1. Centre the rosette (E) in the middle of the cross and weld in place.
2. Centre the scroll set (F) over the rosette. Bend the arrow tips upward until the scroll set makes contact with all four arms. Weld in place.

Mark the midpoint of both vertical base ends and one end of each horizontal base. Mark 1" from the ends. Connect the marks at a diagonal to create a point.

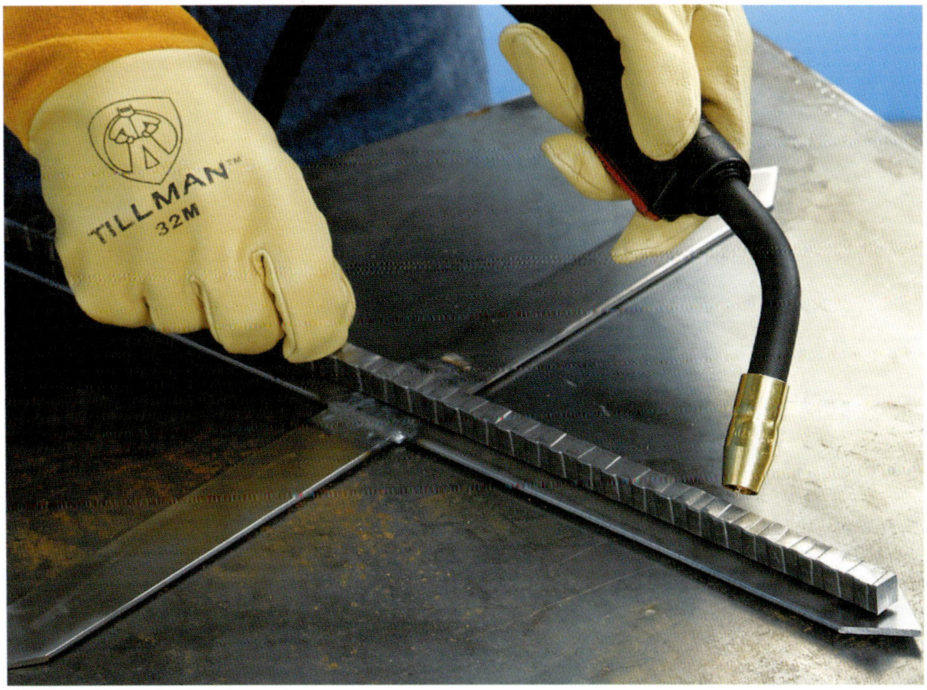

Centre the vertical top on the vertical base and weld in place with 2 to 3 welds per side.

Drill mounting holes through the vertical base. Use machine oil and a slow drill speed to preserve the drill bit.

3. Centre the finials (G) on the bar ends and weld in place.

FINISH THE CROSS

1. Drill $\frac{3}{16}$" mounting holes through the vertical base on either side of the top bar and about 1" from the top and bottom (see photo).
2. Wire brush or sandblast the cross. Finish as desired.
3. Because of the weight of the cross, make sure it is mounted on a wall stud. Hang the cross with $1\frac{1}{2}$" screws.

Nesting Tables

Do you like to entertain but find that you're constantly searching for extra tables as the guests arrive? Nesting tables are the perfect way to always be ready to entertain on the fly. Best of all, they can be tucked away at the end of the evening. The basic pattern here is for three tabletops. These tables have wooden tops with a ½" overhang. You may adjust the measurements for tile or metal tops. If you want the tables to nest even closer, use ½" angle iron with a 16-gauge or ⅛" metal top. And don't forget to dress these tables up! Consider using hammered bar or adding decorative elements to the legs to allow them to show off a bit at parties.

MATERIALS

- ½ × ½" square bar (28 feet)
- 1 × 1 × ⅛" angle iron (17 feet)
- ½" handipanel or veneered plywood (2 ft. × 4 ft. sheet)
- ¾" #8 panhead screws (12)

Top view of tabletop frames

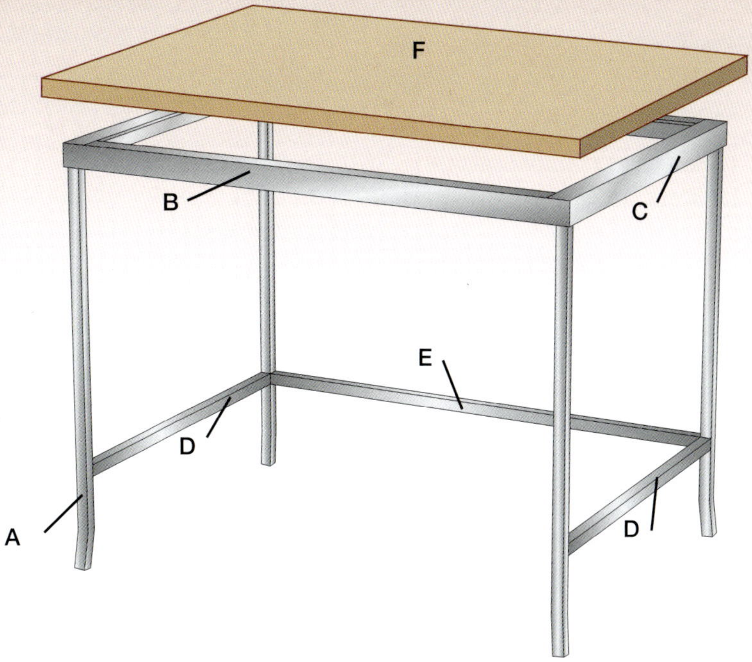

LARGE TABLE

PART	NAME	DIMENSIONS	QUANTITY
A	Legs	½ × ½" square bar × 18"	4
B	Table long sides	1 × 1 × ⅛" angle iron × 23"	2
C	Table short sides	1 × 1 × ⅛" angle iron × 17"	2
D	Crossbars	½ × ½" square bar × 15¾"	2
E	Back bar	½ × ½" square bar × 21¾"	1
F	Wood tabletop	24 × 18"	1

MEDIUM TABLE

PART	NAME	DIMENSIONS	QUANTITY
A	Legs	½ × ½" square bar × 16"	4
B	Table long sides	1 × 1 × ⅛" angle iron × 20"	2
C	Table short sides	1 × 1 × ⅛" angle iron × 14"	2
D	Crossbars	½ × ½" square bar × 12¾"*	2
E	Back bar	½ × ½" square bar × 18¾"*	1
F	Wood tabletop	21 × 15"	1

SMALL TABLE

PART	NAME	DIMENSIONS	QUANTITY
A	Legs	½ × ½" square bar × 14"	4
B	Table long sides	1 × 1 × ⅛" angle iron × 17"	2
C	Table short sides	1 × 1 × ⅛" angle iron × 11"	2
D	Crossbars	½ × ½" square bar × 9¾"	2
E	Back bar	½ × ½" square bar × 15¾"	1
F	Wood tabletop	18 × 12"	1

* Approximate dimensions, cut to fit.

How to Build Nesting Tables

Before welding, thoroughly clean all parts with denatured alcohol.

Make the Legs

1. Cut the legs of the large table (A) to length.
2. Clamp the lower 1½" of a leg into a sturdy bench vise. Slide a 3-ft. length of ½" pipe over the leg. Bend it about 5°.
3. Using the first leg as a template, bend all the remaining legs to match.
4. Repeat Steps 1 to 3 with the medium and small tables.

Make the Tabletop Frames

1. Cut the table long sides (B) and table short sides (C) to length. Mitre the ends at 45°, or cut notches in the long sides, as shown (see top photo, below).
2. Lay out one long side and one short side of the large table, using a carpenter's square to check for square. Clamp into place and tack-weld the corner (see photo, below).
3. Repeat Step 2 with the other long and short sides.
4. Use a carpenter's square to align the two Ls to form a rectangle.
5. Weld the outside joints together. Grind down the welds.
6. Repeat Steps 1 to 5 with the medium and small tables.

Using a carpenter's square, lay out the table sides. Tack-weld together and check for square before final welding.

For a wood or metal tabletop, weld the legs inside the corner formed by the flanges. Align the curved legs so they point toward the long sides.

Attach the Legs

If you will be making a wooden or metal tabletop, turn the table frame so the flanges of the angle iron are pointing downward. Weld the legs inside the corner (see bottom photo, left). If you will be making a tile tabletop, turn the frame so the flanges are pointing up, to create a cradle for the base and tile. Weld the legs to the bottom of the frame (see bottom photo, opposite page).

1. Place a leg on or in a corner, with the bend facing the long side. Use a carpenter's square to check that it is square from front to back and side to side. Weld in place.
2. Repeat Step 1 with the remaining legs.
3. Measure the distance between the legs on the short sides, close to the frame. Cut the crossbars (D) to fit. Weld the crossbars into place at 4" from the bottom of the legs.
4. Measure the distance between the legs on a long side, close to the frame. Cut the back bar (E) to fit. Weld into place, even with the crossbars.
5. Repeat Steps 1 to 4 with the medium and small tables.
6. Grind down all the welds. Sand, wire brush, or sandblast the tables. Finish as desired. (If using a metal top, install it before finishing.)

OPTION 1: CREATE A WOOD TOP

The wood tabletops have a $\frac{1}{2}$" overhang.

1. Cut the wood tabletop (F) to size.
2. If using a Handipanel, sand the edges smooth, slightly rounding the top edge and corners, or use a $\frac{1}{2}$" roundover bit and rout the edges.
3. If the top is veneered plywood, apply edge banding with an iron. Trim the banding to fit and lightly sand the edges and corners.
4. Apply paint, stain, or finish.
5. Turn the table upside down and drill a $\frac{3}{16}$" hole in each side. Drill a corresponding $\frac{1}{8}$" pilot hole in the underside of the tabletop (see bottom photo, right). Attach the top to the table with $\frac{3}{4}$" panhead screws.
6. Repeat Steps 1 to 5 with the medium and small tables.

After drilling holes in each of the table's sides, align the wood top and drill pilot holes for the mounting screws.

OPTION 2: CREATE A TILE TOP

1. Measure the inside dimension of the tabletop. Cut $\frac{3}{4}$" exterior-grade plywood to fit.
2. Mark the plywood piece with your desired tile layout.
3. Apply a small amount of silicone adhesive to the lip of the table. Place the plywood onto the table.
4. Apply a layer of adhesive to the back of each tile using a notched trowel. Place the tiles on the plywood according to your pattern. After placing the tiles, use a carpet-covered 2 × 4 and a rubber mallet to set the tiles.
5. After the adhesive sets, apply grout to the tile spaces according to manufacturer's instructions. Do not apply grout to the gap between the metal frame and the tiles. Use colored silicone sealant between the metal and the tiles.
6. Repeat Steps 1 to 5 with the medium and small tables.

For a tiled tabletop, weld the legs to the flat underside—so that the flanges form a cradle for the tile and backing material.

OPTION 3: CREATE A METAL TOP

You can make a metal top of matching steel, or create a contrasting look with expanded sheet metal, patterned stainless steel, or aluminum. A glass panel covering patterned metal creates a smooth surface while allowing the pattern to shine through.

1. Cut the metal to fit the dimensions of the table.
2. Tack-weld the top to the table from the underside, or weld around the entire perimeter. Grind the contact points to create a smooth transition.
3. Repeat Steps 1 and 2 with the medium and small tables.

Tapered-Leg Table

Here's a whimsical table that is fun to make if you have access to a plasma cutter. The tapered legs with curled ends provide a delicate touch. Although it's not a sturdy table, its light and airy graces make it perfect for small plants or curios. The curls on the legs turn out on this table but are equally as intriguing when turned inward. You could also make a nesting set. The welds holding this table together are all on the bottom or inside surfaces. An angle grinder was used to achieve the finish. Simply grind strips of about 1 × 2" in a circular motion until you get the right texture. If you want smooth joints for a painted finish, weld from the outside and grind the welds smooth.

Materials

- ⅛" sheet metal (6 × 30" rectangle, 12" square)
- ⅛ × 2" flat bar (2½ feet)
- ½" black pipe (6")

PART	NAME	DIMENSIONS	QUANTITY
A	Legs	⅛" sheet metal × 3" × 30"	3
B	Top	⅛" sheet metal × 12 × 12 right triangle	1
C	Front skirt	⅛" × 2" flat bar × 12"*	1
D	Side skirts	⅛" × 2" flat bar × 7"*	2

* Approximate dimensions, cut to fit.

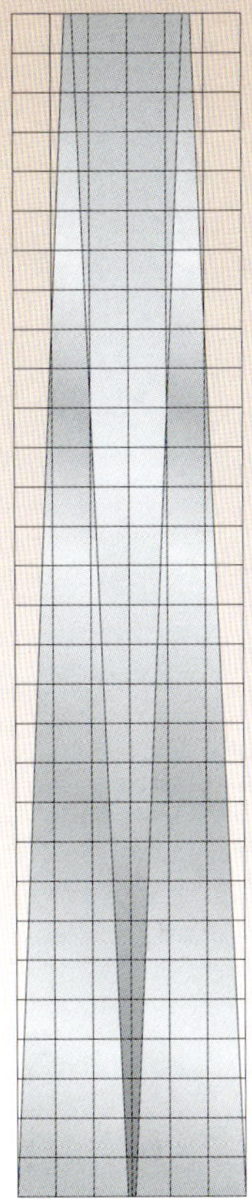

CUTTING DIAGRAM

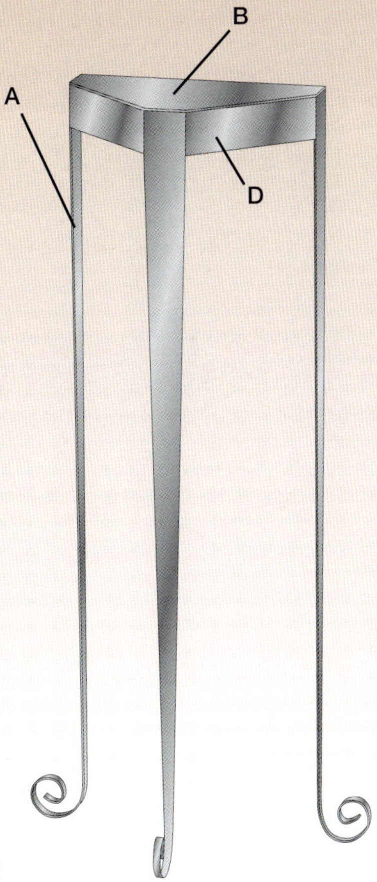

How to Build a Tapered-Leg Table

Before welding, thoroughly clean all parts with denatured alcohol.

CUT THE LEGS

1. Mark the 6 × 30" rectangle at 3" on one 6" end and at 1½" and 4½" at the opposite end.
2. Using a long straightedge, draw diagonal lines connecting the marks to create triangles (see diagram).
3. Cut along the lines using a plasma cutter or oxyacetylene torch to create the legs (A).
4. Remove slag and grind off any cutting imperfections on the three triangles.
5. Cut a ⅛" notch in a piece of black pipe and insert the pipe in a bench vise.
6. Insert about ¼" of the pointed end of the triangle into the notch and bend slightly. Insert more of the leg and bend again. Continue inserting and bending until the point contacts the opposite side (see photo, right).
7. Bend the leg around the outside of the pipe one full turn.
8. Bend the remaining two legs, using the first leg as a pattern. If the notch in the black pipe gets sloppy or the pipe sides splay, cut off the notched end and cut a new notch.
9. Adjust the scrolls so that all three legs are the same length.

CUT THE TOP

1. Cut the 12" square in half diagonally to create the triangular top (B).
2. To determine the exact cut off lengths for the points of the top, lay one leg on top of the triangle at each point. Mark cutting lines on the top where the legs overlap, but don't overhang the top. (This will be about 3" in from the 45° corners and about 1½" in from the 90° corner.)
3. Cut the corners off the top using a plasma cutter or oxyacetylene torch.
4. With the tabletop lying flat, align a leg with a corner so it is standing perpendicular to the top. Tack-weld in place from the inside. Repeat with the other two legs.

COMPLETE THE TABLE

1. Measure between the legs to determine the lengths of the front and side skirts (C and D). Cut the skirts to length.
2. Tack-weld the skirts to the legs and top from the inside.
3. Stand the table upright to check for alignment. Make adjustments and finish the welds.
4. Wire brush and clean with denatured alcohol. Finish as desired.

Cut a ⅛" notch in a ½" black pipe. Bend the scrolls by incrementally inserting the pointed end into the notch and bending. Once the point has reached the opposite side of the pipe, bend the leg around the outside of the pipe one full turn.

Swing-Away Coat Hooks

These good-looking, easy-to-make coat hooks are considerably sturdier than those you might purchase at discount stores. The pivoting design lets them fold flat against the wall when not in use, so you can install them wherever you want.

Customize the hooks with a special shaped back plate or use cut out letters to personalize hooks for a child's room. Make the hooks shorter, if desired, or use more than three hooks. Mount the hooks on a stud to prevent the weight of coats from pulling them out of the wall.

Materials

- 16-gauge ½" round tube (9")
- ¼" round rod (10")
- 3⁄16" round rod (6½ feet)
- ⅛ × 2" flat bar (12")
- 1" O.D. ball ¼" 20 threaded (2, Decorative Iron #C50035)

PART	NAME	DIMENSIONS	QUANTITY
A	Hooks	3⁄16" round rod × 9"*	3
B	Crossbars	3⁄16" round rod × 7"*	3
C	Scrolls	3⁄16" round rod × 9"	3
D	Barrels	16-gauge ½" round tube × 3"	3
E	Pin	¼" round rod × 10"	1
F	Balls	1" round balls	2
G	Back plate	⅛ × 2" flat bar × 12"	1

* Approximate dimensions, cut to fit.

How to Build Swing-Away Coat Hooks

Before welding, thoroughly clean all parts with denatured alcohol.

MAKE THE SCROLLS

1. Cut the scroll blanks (C) to length. Round the rod ends with a grinder.
2. Clamp one end of the scroll blank to a ½" pipe. Bend the scroll around the pipe a ¾ turn.
3. Clamp the other end of the scroll to a 1" pipe. Bend the scroll around the pipe a ¾ turn in the opposite direction.
4. Repeat with the other two scrolls, matching the bends in the first scroll.

MAKE THE HOOKS

1. Cut the hooks and crossbars (A and B) to length. Round one hook end with a grinder.
2. Place 1" of the hook into a bench vise and bend to about 110°. Repeat with the other two hooks.
3. Align a crossbar at 90° to the hook and weld in place (see photo).
4. Trim the hook and crossbar ends to match, if necessary.
5. Place a scroll between the legs of a hook. The hook legs should be no more than 2¾" apart.
6. Arrange the other hooks and scrolls to match the first. Weld together.

MAKE THE HINGE

1. Cut the barrels (D) to length. Draw a guideline down the centre of each barrel. Make a mark at ½" down from the top of each barrel along the guideline.
2. Align the hook with the barrel so the upper leg of the hook is at the intersection of the guideline and the ½" mark.
3. Weld the hook legs to the barrel.
4. Repeat Steps 2 and 3 with the other two hooks.
5. Cut the pin (E) to length. Grind down ½" at each end of the pin to fit the holes in the balls. Slide the barrels over the pin. Place the balls (F) over the pin at each end.

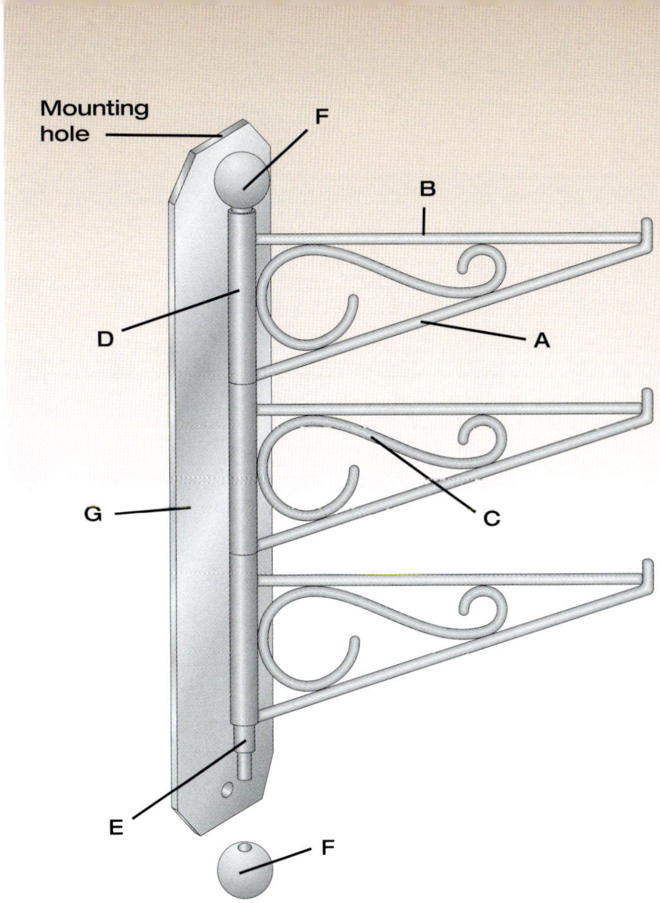

ASSEMBLE THE COAT HOOKS

1. Cut the back plate (G) to size. Round the corners with a grinder.
2. Drill ⁵⁄₃₂" mounting holes centred 1" from each end.
3. Measure the distance between the centres of the balls on the hook assembly. Drill ¼" holes this distance apart on the centreline of the back plate.
4. Place the hook assembly on the back so the balls rest in the holes. From the back side, weld the balls to the back plate.
5. Sand, wire brush, or sandblast the coat hooks. Finish as desired.

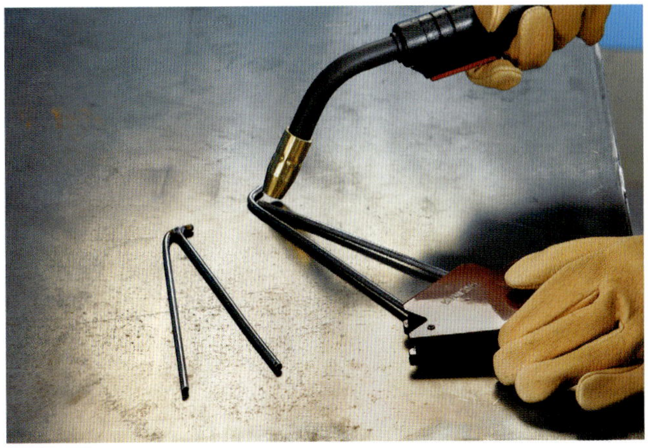

Align the crossbar with the hook and weld the ends together. A magnetic clamp helps hold the small parts in place.

INCIDENTAL TABLE WITH DRAWER

Sleek and sophisticated, this table may be designed like a wood table, but its unmatched style comes from metal. Many people find metal easier to work with than wood, and metal can offer the same great looks without all that sawdust.

When working with thinner materials, make sure to turn your welder to the appropriate setting to prevent burn through and distortion.

PART	NAME	DIMENSIONS	QUANTITY
A	Legs	16-gauge 1 x 1" square tube x 22"	4
B	Table frames	16-gauge 1 x 1" square tube x 20"	4
C	Shelf	16-gauge sheet metal x 14 x 20"*	1
D	Drawer box	22-gauge sheet metal x 18 x 6"	1
E	Drawer glides	16-gauge ½ x ½" angle iron x 18"	2
F	Drawer face	16-gauge sheet metal x 6 x 12*	1
G	Sides	16-gauge sheet metal x 18 x 6"	2
H	Back	16-gauge sheet metal x 12 x 6"	1
I	Bars	⅛ x ½" flat bar x 11"*	13
J	Tabletop	16-gauge sheet metal x 20 x 20"*	1
K	Drawer handle		1

*Approximate dimensions, cut to fit.

MATERIALS

- 16-gauge 1 × 1" square tube (14½ feet)
- 16-gauge sheet metal (3 ft. × 5½ ft. sheet)
- 16-gauge andle iron (3 feet)
- ⅛ × ½" flat bar (14 feet)
- 22-gauge sheet metal (2 ft. × 1 ft. sheet)
- Drawer handle

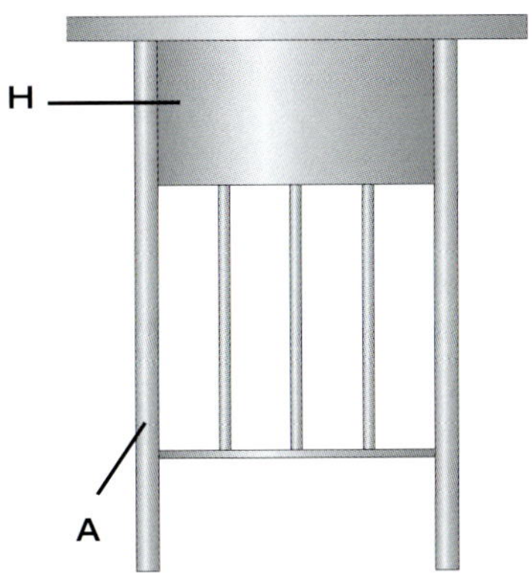

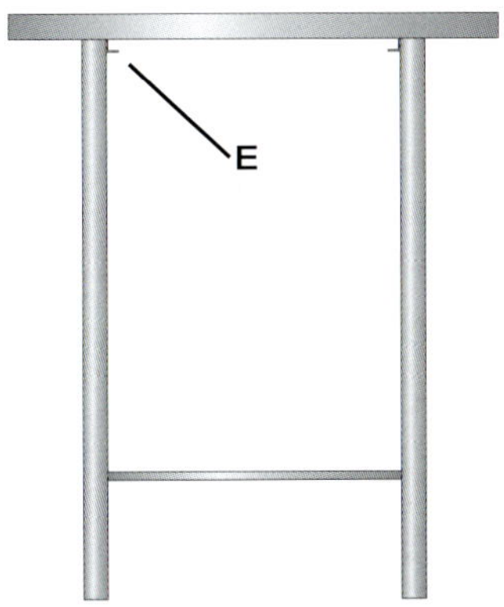

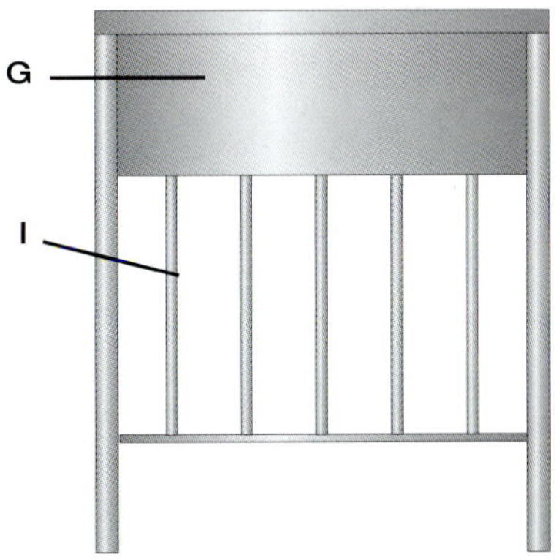

Top view

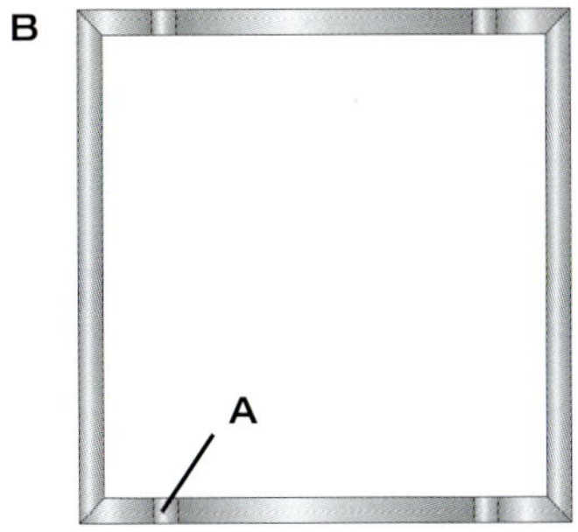

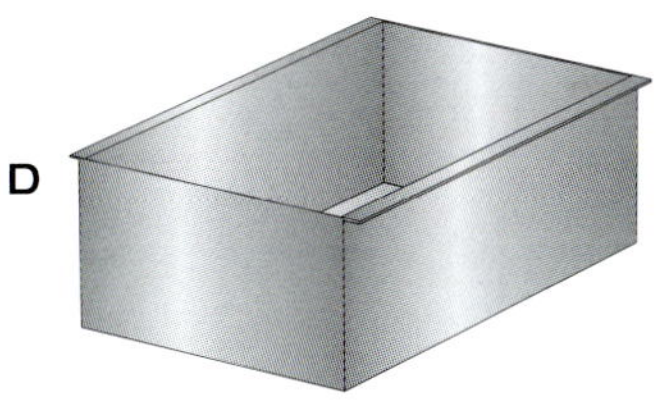

How to Build an Incidental Table with Drawer

Before welding, thoroughly clean all parts with denatured alcohol.

MAKE THE TABLE FRAME

1. Cut the legs (A) and table frame (B) to size. Mitre the frame ends at 45°.
2. On a flat work surface, position two sides of the frame in an L shape. Use a carpenter's square to check for square and then clamp in place. Tack-weld the corner. Repeat with the other two sides.
3. Arrange the two Ls to make a square. Clamp in place. Measure across the diagonals to check for square. If the diagonal measurements are not equal, the assembly is not square. Adjust and recheck. Tack-weld the corners.
4. After rechecking for square, finish welding all the joints.
5. Grind down the welds to be flush with the surrounding metal.
6. Mark points 3" in from the ends on one frame side. Mark points 3" in from the ends on the opposite frame side.
7. Align a leg with the mark and tack-weld into place. Use clamps and angle iron to securely hold the leg (see photo, below). Repeat with the other three legs.
8. Make sure the legs are perpendicular to the frame and weld in place.

Clamp a leg in place with a piece of angle iron and two C clamps. Check for square and weld the leg to the table frame.

MAKE THE SHELF

1. Before cutting the shelf (C) to size, measure between the outside faces of the front and side legs to make sure this dimension is correct. Cut the shelf to size.
2. Make 1 × 1" cutouts in each corner of the shelf, using a plasma cutter, oxyacetylene torch, or bandsaw. Note that the square tube has slightly rounded edges, so round the cutouts to match.
3. Mark each leg at 5" from the bottom.
4. Align the shelf with the marks and tack-weld in place. Make sure the shelf is level before finish welding.

MAKE THE DRAWER

1. Cut the drawer (D) to size.
2. Use a hand seamer to bend the drawer sides at 3/8" to 90°.
3. Bend the sides and ends of the drawer to 90° to make a box (see top photo, opposite page).
4. Weld the seams.

FINISH THE DRAWER

1. Measure the distance between the two front legs. Subtract 1/8" and cut the drawer face (F) to size.

2. With the drawer in the frame, place the drawer face over the drawer front. Align the drawer face with a 1⁄16" gap between the frame and legs. Placing magnetic right-angle clamps in the drawer makes this task easier.
3. Tack-weld the drawer face to the drawer from the inside.
4. Remove the drawer and complete the welds.
5. Centre your chosen drawer pull on the drawer face and mark the screw locations. Drill the holes for the pull.

ADD THE SIDES AND BACK

1. Before cutting the sides (G) and back (H), measure between the side legs and the back legs to determine the exact lengths. Cut the back and sides to size.
2. Place the sides and back and weld in place.
3. Measure from the top of the shelf to the bottom of the sides and back to determine the correct length for the bars (I). Cut the bars to length.
4. Place three bars evenly spaced (approximately 3" on center) across the back. Make sure the bars are perfectly vertical before welding. Place five bars evenly spaced (approximately 3" on centre) across each side (see photo, middle). Make sure the bars are perfectly vertical before welding.

FINISH THE TABLE

1. Measure the top outside dimension of the table frame. Cut the tabletop (J) to size using these dimensions.
2. Attach the tabletop from the underside using two small welds per side. If you prefer a tabletop that appears one with the frame, weld around the entire perimeter of the tabletop and grind the weld smooth.
3. Wire brush, sand, or sandblast the table and drawer. Finish as desired.
4. Attach the drawer pull.

MAKE THE DRAWER GLIDES

1. Cut the glides (E) to size.
2. Mark 1⁄4" down from the top inside of each leg. Align the glides with the lines and tack-weld in place (see photo, bottom).
3. Slide the drawer into the frame and check for fit. Adjust if necessary, and complete the welds.

Cut the drawer to size. Clamp the drawer to a sharp-edged surface using C clamps and a piece of angle iron. Bend the sides, back and front of the drawer to 90°.

Weld the decorative bars to the table sides and shelf every 3". Weld from the inside.

Weld the drawer glides to the legs.

PART	NAME	DIMENSIONS	QUANTITY
A	Legs	16-gauge 1 × 1" square tube × 68"	4
B	Side crossbars	16-gauge 1 × 1" square tube × 19"	4
C	Centre supports	16-gauge 1 × 1" square tube × 66"*	2
D	Side horizontals	16-gauge ½ × ½" square tube × 9"*	24
E	Verticals	16-gauge ½ × ½" square tube × 4"	60
F	Circles	4" O.D. square tube rings	20
G	Crossbars	16-gauge 1 × 1" square tube × 39"	3
H	Back horizontals	16-gauge ½ × ½" square tube × 39"	6
I	Shelf supports	16-gauge ½ × ½" square tube × 19"	2
J	Shelf rods	⅛ × ½" flat bar × 39"	12
K	Hanging rod	⅛ × 1" round tube × 39"	1
L	Spheres	1½"	8

Coat Rack

"Welcome to my home—please, let me hang your coat." This ornate coat rack is the perfect way to invite guests into your home. It's convenient for older homes that lack an entryway closet, but don't confuse this rack for any old ordinary hall tree. This is an attractive and sturdy piece of furniture. Styled to complement most early 20th century homes, it consistently draws attention from visitors.

The circular details are created by sawing square tube rings in half and joining them to a vertical post. If you prefer to save time on sawing, simply use the whole ring without the vertical element. Make sure you purchase square tube circles that match the dimensions on the other components.

Materials

- 16-gauge ½ × ½" square tube (58 feet)
- 16-gauge 1 × 1" square tube (50 feet)
- 4" O.D. square tube rings (20, Triple S Steel #SR 4)
- ⅛ × 1" round tube (39")
- ⅛ × ½" flat bar (39 feet)
- 1½" spheres (8, Triple S Steel SF116F4)

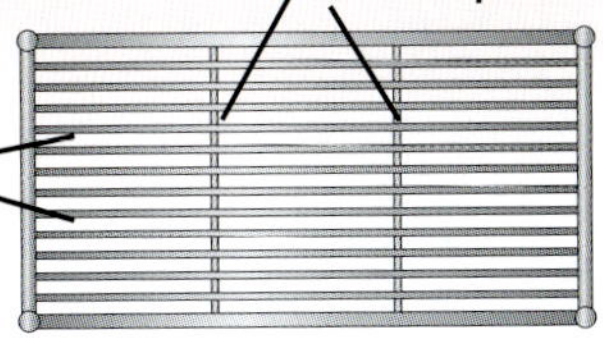

Top view

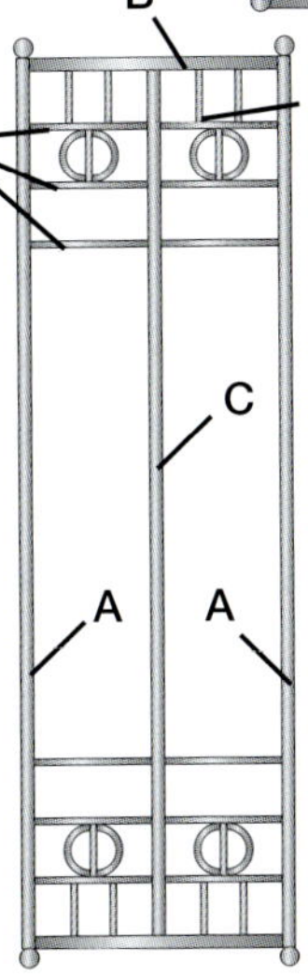

Side view

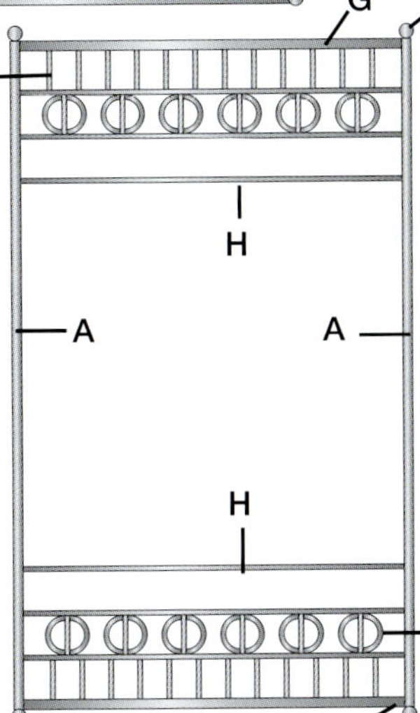

Back view

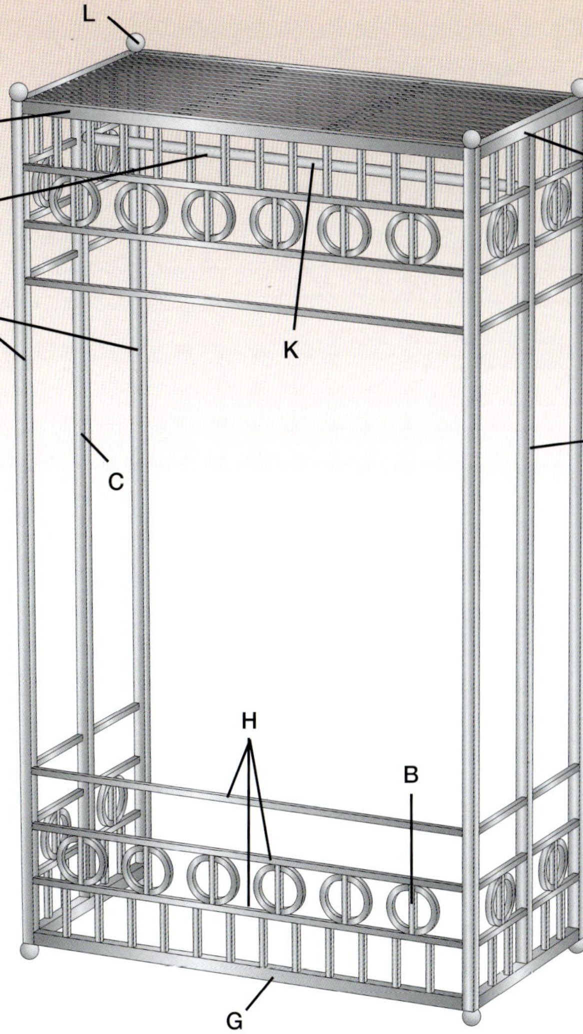

How to Build a Coat Rack

Before welding, thoroughly clean all parts with denatured alcohol.

MAKE THE SIDE PANELS

1. Cut the legs (A) and side crossbars (B) to length.
2. Lay out the crossbars between the legs. Align the crossbars flush with the top and bottom of the legs. Check for square and clamp in place. Tack-weld the corners. Measure across the diagonals. If the two measurements are not equal, adjust the frame and recheck. Complete the welds.
3. Before cutting the centre supports (C), measure the distance between the crossbars (see photo, below). Cut the center supports to this measurement. Centre the supports between the legs; check for square and weld in place.

ADD THE DECORATIVE ELEMENTS

The decorative elements are ½" thick, the legs and supports are 1" thick—this results in the decorations being flush on one side and recessed on the other.

1. Measure between the legs and centre supports and cut the side horizontals (D) to this measurement.
2. Measure the circles' (F) outside diameter. Cut the verticals (E) to this dimension.
3. Cut the circles in half. Create a cradle of wood blocks on plywood backing to make this easier (see left photo, opposite page). Cut through the side opposite the joint. The weld will easily bend apart.
4. Place the side panel on a flat surface and lay out the horizontals. To determine the distance from the crossbars, use the verticals as spacers. Weld the horizontals in place.

Before cutting the centre supports, measure between the crossbars to get the exact dimensions.

Creating a jig to hold the circles in place makes cutting easier. Cut the circles through the side exactly opposite the seam and the weld easily breaks apart.

Weld the decorative elements in place.

5. Place verticals centered at 3" and 6" from the centre support in between the crossbar and the first horizontal. Tack-weld in place.
6. Place verticals centred at 4½" between the second and third horizontals. Tack-weld in place.
7. Place two half circles around the verticals from Step 6. Tack-weld in place (see photo, above right).

ASSEMBLE THE COAT RACK

1. Cut the crossbars (G) to length.
2. Stand a side panel on its back leg with the flush side facing outward. Align a crossbar with the top of the leg, check for square, and tack-weld in place.
3. Align a second crossbar flush with the bottom of the leg, check for square, and tack-weld in place.
4. Align the second side panel with the crossbars; check for square and tack-weld in place.
5. Align the third crossbar flush with the tops of the front legs. Tack-weld in place.
6. Measure the diagonals across the back. Both diagonals should be equal. Measure the diagonals across the top. Both diagonals should be equal. If measurements are not equal, adjust as necessary. When the unit is square, complete the welds.

DECORATE THE BACK

1. Cut the back horizontals (H) to length. Use verticals as spacers to align the horizontals between the legs, and weld in place.
2. Place the verticals centered at 3" intervals between the crossbars and the first horizontal. Weld in place.
3. Starting at 4½", place verticals centered at 6" intervals between the first and second horizontals. Weld in place.
4. Place two half circles around each vertical from Step 3. Weld in place.

FINISH THE COAT RACK

If you plan on storing objects heavier than hats and gloves on top of the rack, use four supports instead of two.

1. Cut the shelf supports (I) and shelf rods (J) to length.
2. Place the shelf supports between the two top crossbars, evenly spaced. Recess the supports from the top ⅛" and weld in place.
3. Space the shelf pieces 1" apart. Weld the pieces to the side crossbars and shelf supports.
4. Cut the hanging rod (K) to length. Weld it to the centre supports, aligning it even with the first horizontals.
5. Weld the spheres (L) into the ends of the legs.
6. Grind down all welds. Sand, wire brush, or sandblast the coat rack. Finish as desired. A coat of automotive paste wax on the hanging bar will protect the painted surface from damage by hangers.

Scroll Lamp with Table

Making a lamp is a great way to put your welding skills and artistic style to practical use. Many home improvement and craft stores have lamp kits to help with the technical wiring required for this project, so don't let that part scare you off. As the basic lamp constructing process eases over time, you're left with pure imagination to customize new lamps in the future.

The reading lamp in this project has a quaint wood tabletop that adds a warm, rich touch, making it suitable for a bedside table or a spot next to your favorite reading chair. Depending on your style preference, the table may be supported by simple S-scrolls or ornately decorated scrolls. Architectural Iron Designs #69/41 is a flat bar scroll with a crimp.

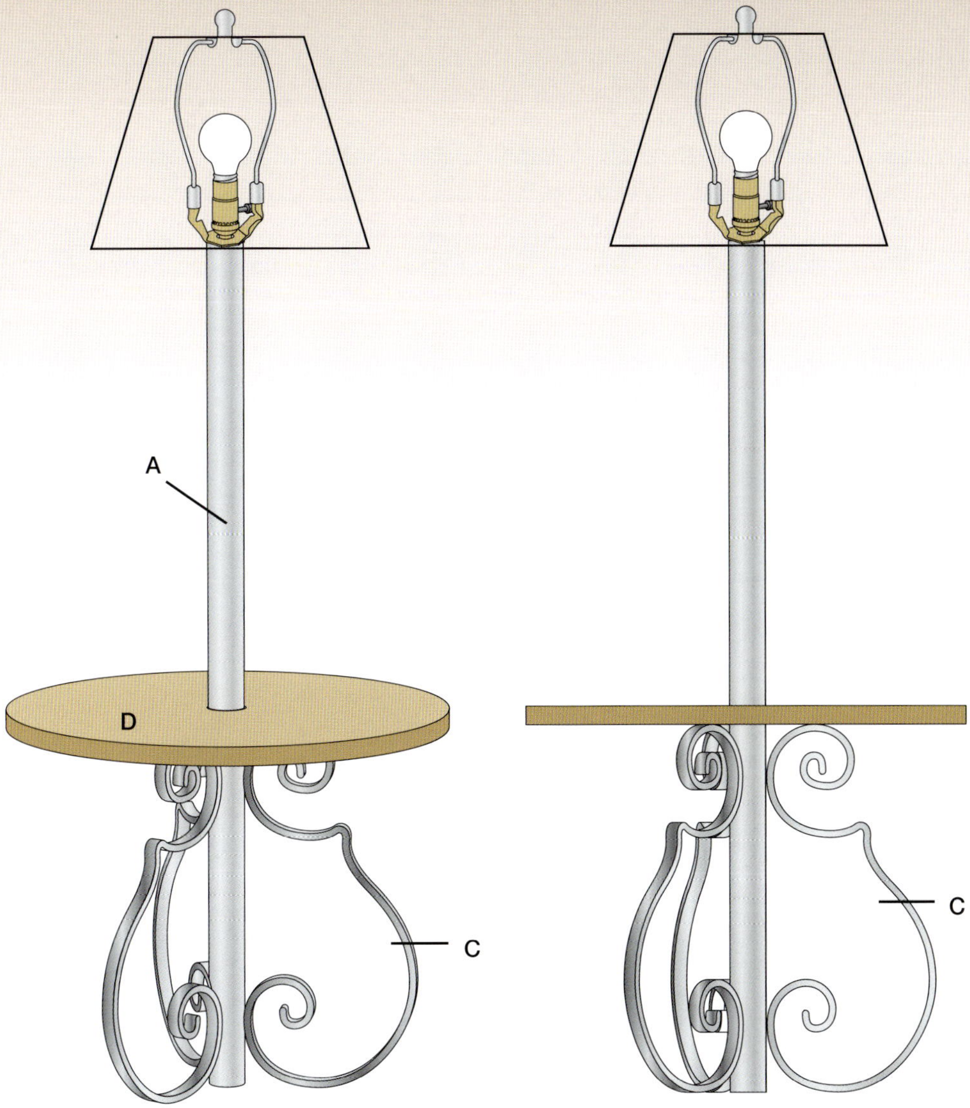

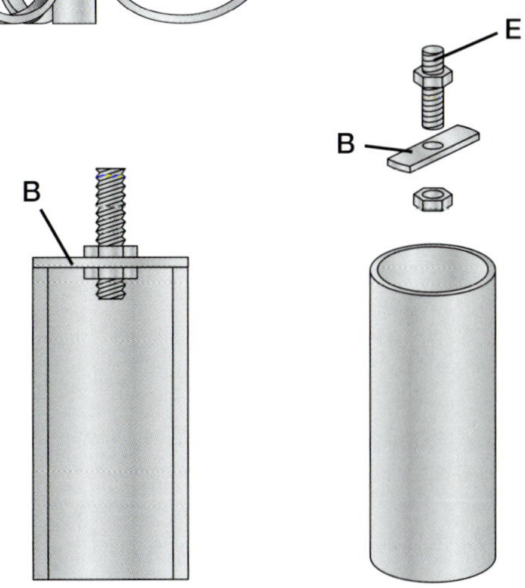

MATERIALS

- 16-gauge 2" round tube (46")
- 3/4 × 3/8" square scrolls (3, Architectural Iron Designs #69/41)
- 3/4" veneer plywood (24 × 24")
- 1/8 × 1/2" flat bar (2")
- Lamp hardware
- Lamp shade
- 3/8" hollow threaded rod and nuts
- Veneer edge banding (6 feet)

PART	NAME	DIMENSIONS	QUANTITY
A	Post	16-gauge 2" round tube × 46"	1
B	Crosspiece	1/8 × 1/2" flat bar × 2"	1
C	Scrolls	17–20"	3
D	Tabletop	3/4" veneer plywood (22" diameter circle)	1
E	Rod	3/8" hollow threaded rod and nuts	1

How to Build a Scroll Lamp with Table

Make the Lamp

Before welding, thoroughly clean all parts with denatured alcohol.

1. Cut the post (A) to length. Cut the crosspiece (B) to length. Round the crosspiece ends to fit the curve of the pipe.
2. Drill a 5⁄16" hole at the centre point of the crosspiece.
3. Insert the threaded rod through the hole and thread nuts onto each end. Tighten the nuts, leaving the majority of threaded rod protruding from one side of the crosspiece.
4. Weld the crosspiece to the top of the post with the longer end of the threaded rod pointing up (see photo, below). Grind down the welds.
5. Mark around the circumference of the post at 120° intervals. (Or the 12:00, 4:00, and 8:00 positions.) Clamp the post about ½" above the floor in an upright position, centred over the pattern. Align one scroll (C) with the first mark (see photo, opposite left). Make sure the scroll is vertical. Tack-weld in place.
6. Align the second scroll with the second mark. Tack-weld into place. Reclamp the post, if necessary, and tack-weld the third scroll in place.
7. Unclamp the post. The lamp post should be perpendicular to the floor. If not, adjust the scrolls as necessary. Finish the welds.

Make the Table

Cut the circular tabletop using a plunge router, trammel jig, and straight bit.

1. Mark the center of the 24 × 24" tabletop (D).

Assemble the threaded rod, nuts, and crosspiece. Weld the crosspiece to the top of the lamp post.

2. Set up the trammel to cut an 11" radius and attach the jig to the centre point.
3. Set the router depth to ⅛" and make the first pass.
4. Cut successive ½" passes until the circle is complete.
5. Attach edge banding to the tabletop and trim as necessary.
6. Drill a 2½" hole in the centre of the table, using a hole saw.
7. Sand the tabletop and finish as desired.

WIRE THE LAMP

You can pick up a lamp wiring kit at most home improvement centers.

1. Thread a thin wire or string through the threaded rod from the top. Tape or tie the cord to the wire and pull it through the threaded rod.
2. Thread the wires through the lamp socket and thread the lamp socket base onto the threaded rod.
3. Split the the cord wires in two. Remove about 1" of the insulation. Note: Use wire size #12 (20 amps, 120 volts) or #14 (15 amps, 120 volts).
4. Tie an underwriter's knot and wrap the leads around the terminals (see diagram).
5. Place the black (hot) wire on the dark screw, and the white (neutral) wire covered with rigid insulation on the light-colored screw. The wider prong is neutral.
6. Fit the socket assembly and insulator over those parts.

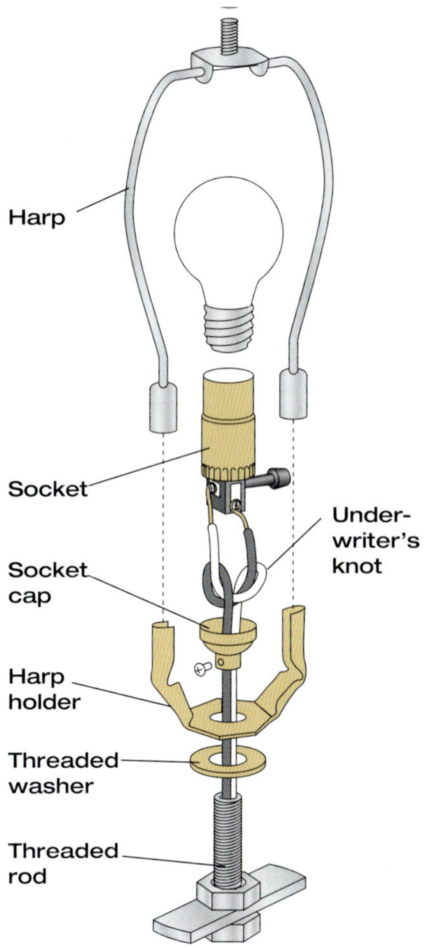

LAMP HARDWARE

Clamp the lamp post upright, about ½" above the floor and over the centre of the pattern. Check for plumb and align the first scroll with the pattern.

Use a router and a trammel jig to cut the circular tabletop.

Votive Lantern with Chain and Holder

Create the perfect evening mood on your patio or deck this summer with soft candlelight. This glass-enclosed lantern protects the flame from breezes, but the small open spaces above the door allow for wafting candle scents. Use a jasmine candle for romance, vanilla for friendship, lemon for entertaining, or citronella to keep those bugs at a distance. You can hang this lantern from a porch ceiling or pergola, or make the hanger base to place the lantern on a tabletop or the floor. To line your garden paths or patio walkways, simply make the stand arm longer and use it as a hanger.

Making this votive lantern will develop your skills in cutting, bending, and welding thin material. Turn your welder down to prevent burn-through—it is best not to use flux-cored wire because it is too hot for the 22-gauge material. Most large home centers carry sheet metal in the 6 x 18" sizes, which makes for less cutting.

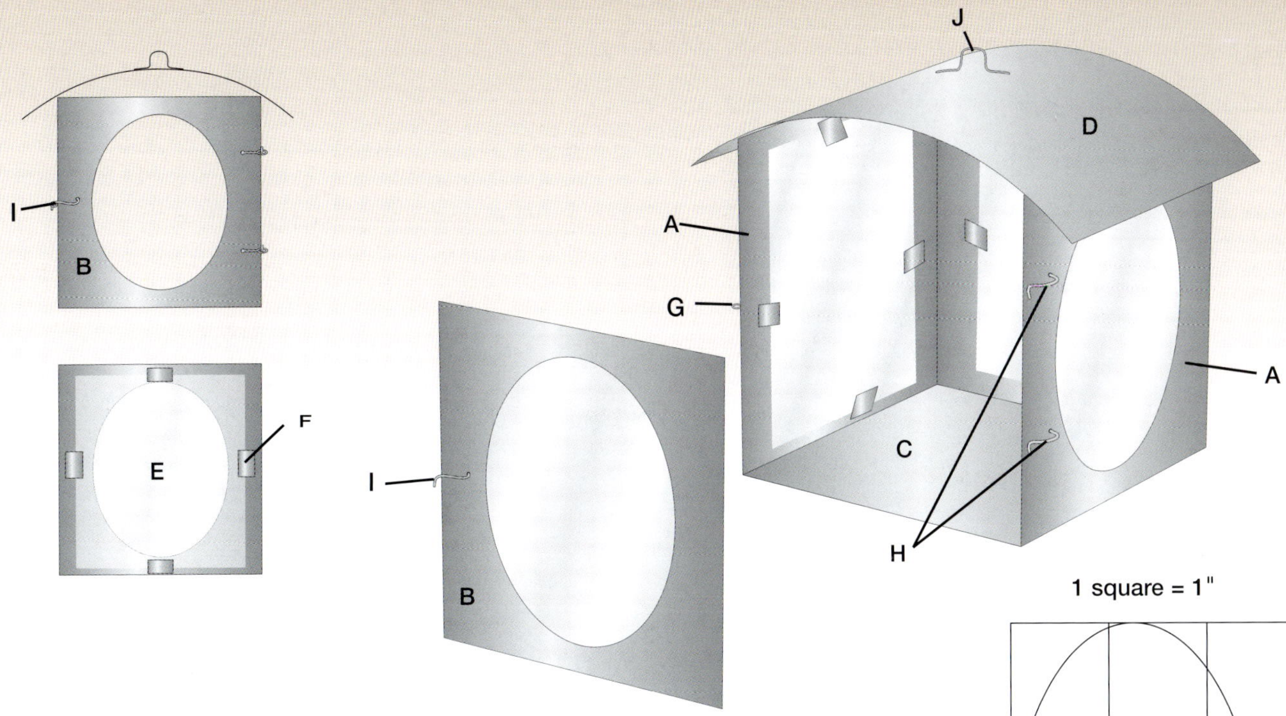

1 square = 1"

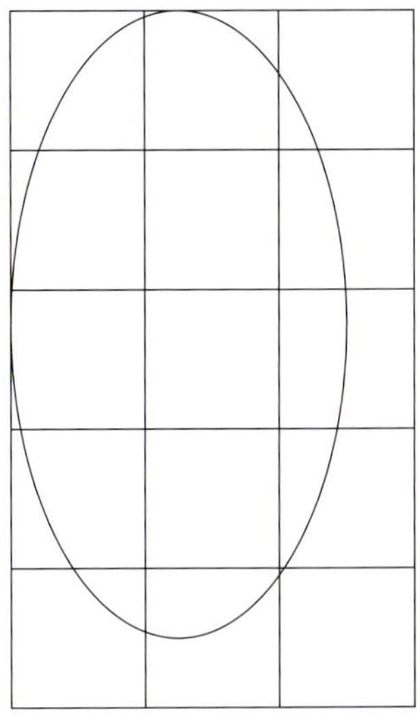

OVAL TEMPLATE

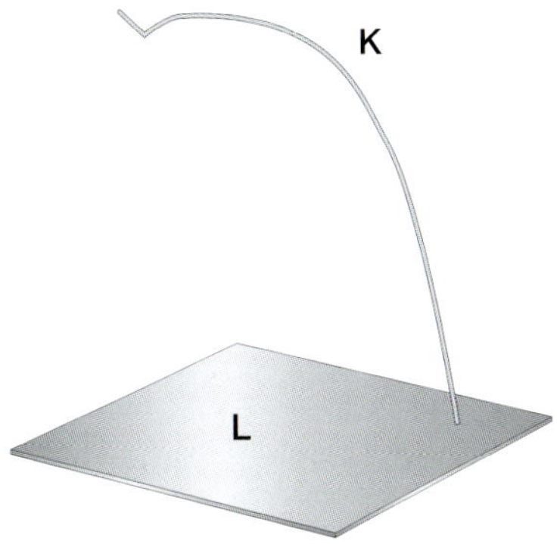

MATERIALS

- 22-gauge sheet metal (3, 6 × 18" sheets)
- Glass (7 × 11")
- ⅛" round rod (4 feet)
- ¼" round rod (26")
- $\frac{3}{16}$" sheet metal (10 × 10")
- Hardwood stick
- 1¼" wire nails (7)

PART	NAME	DIMENSIONS	QUANTITY
A	Sides	22-gauge sheet metal × 6 × 18"	1
B	Door	22-gauge sheet metal × 6 × 6"	1
C	Base	22-gauge sheet metal × 6 × 6"	1
D	Top	22-gauge sheet metal × 9 × 6"	1
E	Glass	3½ × 5½"	4
F	Tabs	22-gauge sheet metal × ¾"*	12
G	Eyelets	1¼" wire nails	3
H	Hinges	1¼" wire nails	3
I	Hook	1¼" wire nail	1
J	Hanger	⅛" round rod × 2"	1
K	Arm	¼" round rod × 26"	1
L	Stand base	$\frac{3}{16}$" sheet metal × 10 × 10"	1
M	Chain	⅛" round rod × 36"	

*Cut to fit.

How to Build a Votive Lantern with Chain and Holder

Before welding, thoroughly clean all parts with denatured alcohol.

MAKE THE CUTOUTS AND SIDES

1. Cut an oval template ($2\frac{1}{2} \times 4\frac{1}{2}$") from sturdy paper or cardboard.
2. Mark the 6 × 18" sheet for the sides (A) at 6" and 12". Centre the oval template in each of the three sections and mark the outline with permanent marker or soapstone.
3. Cut out the ovals using a plasma cutter, oxyacetylene torch, or jigsaw.
4. Cut the door (B) to size. Centre the oval template on the door and mark the outline. Cut out the door oval.
5. At the 6" mark, clamp the sides between two pieces of hardwood or metal. Bend the sheet to 90°, creating a three-sided box (see left photo, below).

INSTALL THE GLASS

1. Cut the glass pieces (E) and the tabs (F) to size.
2. Place each of the glass pieces behind an oval cutout (see right photo, below). Mark tab locations at the bottom and sides of the glass. The tabs are designed to hold the glass in place, so make sure the glass is aligned exactly over the oval cutout.
3. Remove the glass and weld the tabs to the marked locations.

MAKE THE HINGES AND LATCH

1. Cut the base (C) to size. Weld the base to the three sides.
2. Cut the heads off three wire nails. Using a needlenose pliers, bend the pointed end into a circle to form an eyelet (G).
3. Bend two wire nails 90°, $\frac{1}{8}$" from the head, to form the hinges (H).
4. Slide a hinge through an eyelet to complete the hinge.
5. Drill a $\frac{1}{8}$" hole in the door $\frac{1}{2}$" from one side at 3".
6. Bend a wire nail 90°, $\frac{1}{8}$" from the head. Bend the pointed end to form a hook (I).
7. Weld the two hinges to the door, and one side opposite the hole.
8. Insert the hook through the hole in the door and weld the third eyelet to the side adjacent to the hook.

Mark the side piece at 6" and 12". Clamp the side, aligned with a mark, to a sharp-edged tabletop using a piece of angle iron. Bend the side to 90°. Unclamp and move the side to the next mark, clamp and bend.

Centre the glass over the cutouts and mark the tab placements. Centre one per side.

ATTACH THE TOP, HANGER, AND FEET

1. Cut the top (D) to size. Bend the top around a 4" pipe to create the arch.
2. Center the top over the sides, with the overhang perpendicular to the sides with hinges (overhang does not hang over door). Weld into place.
3. Cut the hanger (J) to length and bend to match the pattern.
4. Centre the hanger on the crown of the top and weld into place (see photo, below left).

CREATE THE STAND

1. Cut the arm (K) to length.
2. Create a slight bend in the arm.
3. Clamp the arm in a bench vise, 4" from one end, and bend it approximately 90°. Reclamp the same end at 2" and bend in the opposite direction to form a hook.
4. Cut the stand base (L) to size and shape as desired.
5. Align the arm 1" in from one corner. Weld in place.

MAKE THE CHAIN

1. Wrap the round rod for the chain (M) tightly around a 1 x ½" hardwood stick.
2. Clamp the stick long side down. Use a hacksaw to cut down the middle of the wound metal to create rings (see photo, below right).
3. Slide the rings off the stick. Link the rings together to form a chain.
4. Once the rings are assembled, use pliers or a bench vise to close the gaps.

FINISH THE LANTERN

1. Wire brush or sand the lantern, stand, and chain.
2. Prime and paint, as desired.
3. Replace the glass pieces over the cutouts. Carefully bend the tabs over the glass pieces to hold them in place.

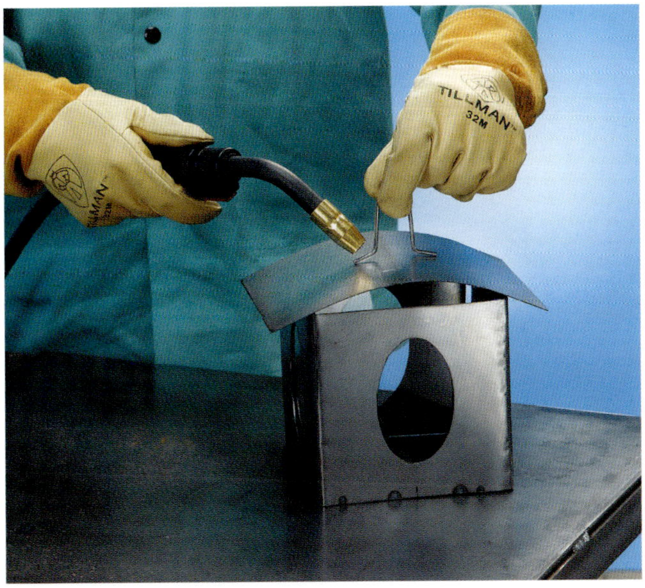

Weld the top to the lantern, then weld the hanger to the top.

Wrap ⅛" round rod around a 1 x ½" hardwood stick. Clamp the stick to a stable surface and cut through the rod on the 1" side to make the individual chain links.

Fireplace Candelabrum

Warm up your hearth, without all the chopping and stacking of wood, with this wavy candelabrum. The simple waves imitate tongues of flames, while the large candleholders support illuminating pillar candles. Romantic, simple, and great for warm summer evenings when a hot fire might be too much.

Materials

- ⅛" sheet metal (13 × 19")
- 4½" bobeches (3, Architectural Iron Designs #79/12)

PART	NAME	DIMENSIONS	QUANTITY
A	Waves	⅛" sheet metal × 4 × 19"	5
B	Bobeches	4½"	3

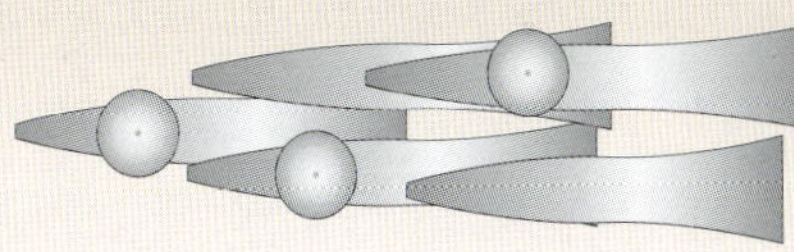

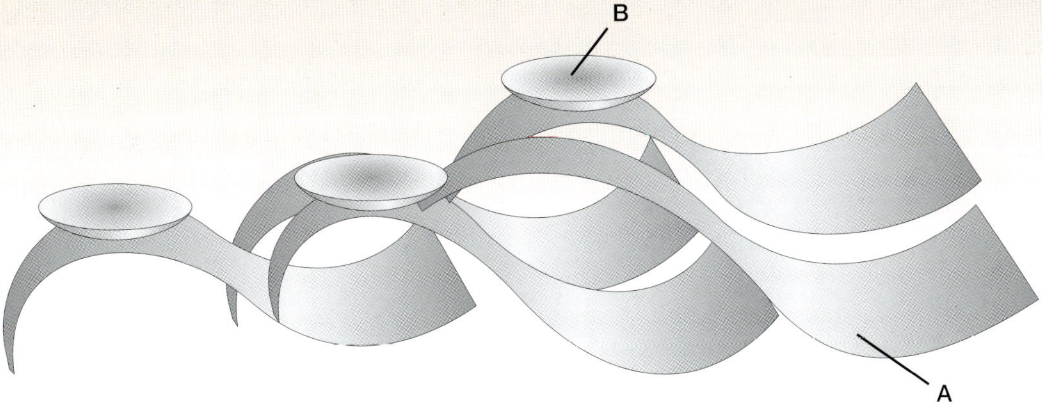

Diagram

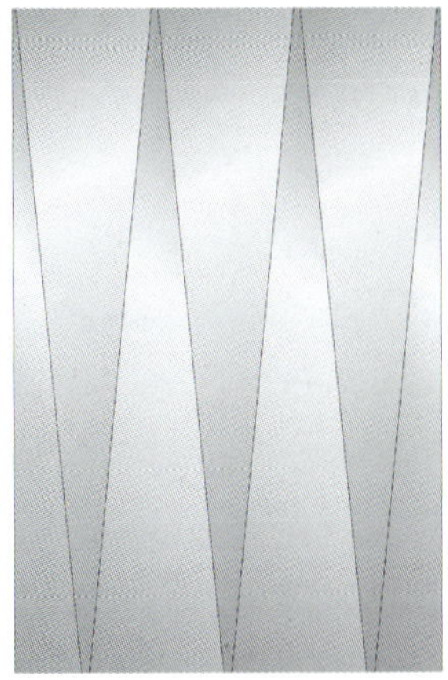

HOW TO BUILD A FIREPLACE CANDELABRUM

Before welding, thoroughly clean all parts with denatured alcohol.

CUT THE WAVES

1. Mark the sheet metal at 4", 4½", 8½", and 9" along one 13" side, and 2", 2½", 6½", 7", 11", and 11½" along the opposite 13" side.
2. Use a straightedge and a permanent marker or soapstone to connect the marks (see diagram).
3. Cut the waves (A) to size using an oxyacetylene torch or plasma cutter.
4. Grind the cut edges smooth, if necessary, and sand or wire brush the metal.

BEND THE WAVES

1. Clamp the narrow end of a wave to a 4" bending form. Bend the wave around just slightly past halfway (see photo).
2. Clamp the wide end of the wave to a 4" bending form. Wrap the wave around the tube a ½ turn in the opposite direction from the first wave.
3. Repeat Steps 1 and 2 with the other four waves.

ARRANGE AND FINISH

1. Arrange the waves as desired. Make sure the arrangement fits in the fireplace.
2. Weld the waves together at the contact points.
3. Place the bobeches on the waves, making sure they are level. Drill a ¼" hole in the centre of each bobeche.
4. Weld the bobeches to the waves by welding through the hole. If you choose to use brass bobeches, braze or braze weld the bobeches to the waves.
5. Finish the candelabrum as desired.

Clamp the narrow wave end to a 4" bending form and bend it slightly past halfway.

HANGING CHANDELIER

Add formal elegance to any room with this timeless chandelier. The acanthus leaf trim is a great conversation piece, and the crystal decorations add a regal flair. You can bend the scrolls with a scroll bender, or form them around rigid circular forms, as we have done here. Bending forms may be constructed from pipe sections, flywheels, sturdy buckets, or ½" plywood. The leaves, candle cups, and crystals are available from catalogue and online sources. To add hangers for more crystals or chains, make a small loop of wire (electrode wire works well) and tack-weld it to the chandelier.

MATERIALS

- 3/16" round rod (24 feet)
- 2 3/8" bobeches (6, Architectural Iron Designs #79/6)
- Candle cups (6, Architectural Iron Designs #78/4)
- 8 1/2" acanthuses (6, Architectural Iron Designs #11942 8 1/2)
- 1" teardrop crystals (24, Chandelierparts)
- 3" hangdrop crystal prisms (5, Chandelierparts)
- 3" teardrop prisms (12, Chandelierparts)

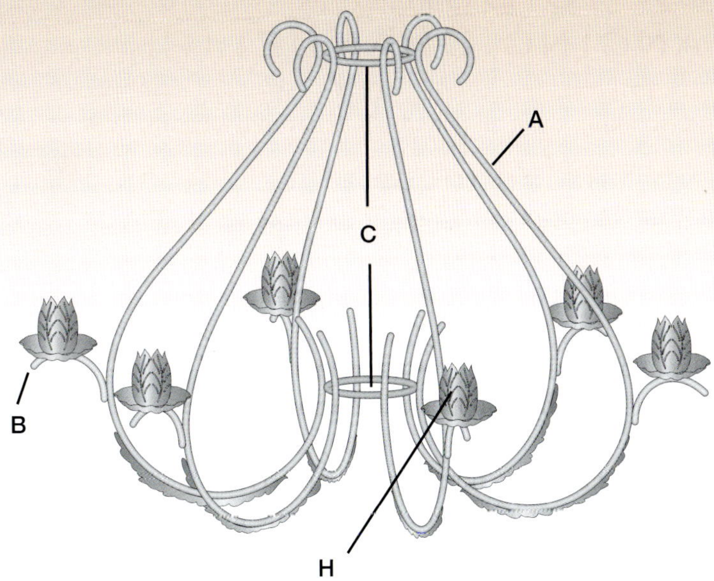

Scroll detail

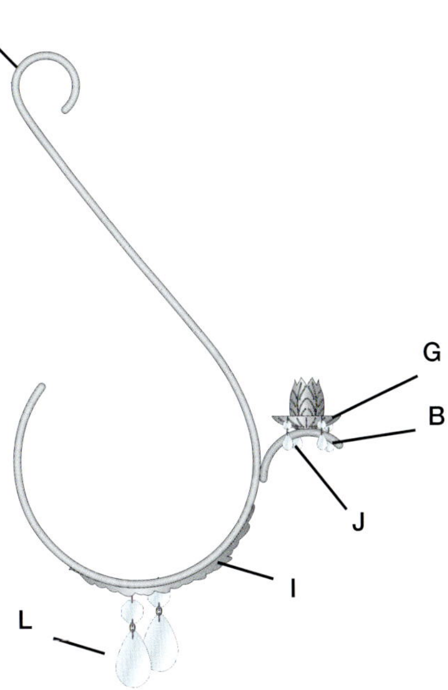

Hanger detail

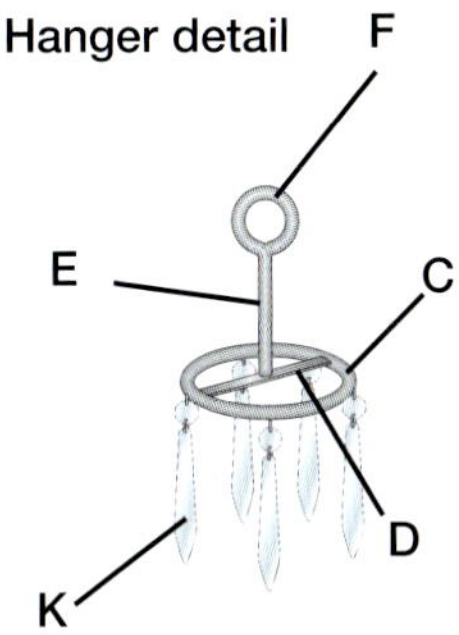

PART	NAME	DIMENSIONS	QUANTITY
A	Scrolls	3/16" round rod × 36"	6
B	Candle arms	3/16" round rod × 3"*	6
C	Rings	3/16" round rod × 9 1/2"*	2
D	Crossbar	3/16" round rod × 3"	1
E	Hanger	3/16" round rod × 6"	1
F	Hanging ring	3/16" round rod × 4"*	1
G	Bobeches (drip trays)	2 3/8"	6
H	Candle cups	1 1/4 × 1 1/4"	6
I	Acanthus leaves	1 1/4 × 8 1/2"	6
J	Teardrop crystals	1"	24
K	Hangdrop crystal prisms	3"	5
L	Teardrop prisms	3"	12

* Approximate dimensions, cut to fit.

HOW TO BUILD A HANGING CHANDELIER

Before welding, clean all parts with denatured alcohol.

BEND THE SCROLLS

1. Cut the scrolls (A) to length. Round the tip of each rod with a grinder.
2. Clamp the opposite end to a 1" form and bend one full turn.
3. Clamp one end to a 4" round form and bend one full turn in the opposite direction (see top photo).
4. Adjust the bends to form a pleasing S scroll.
5. Bend the remaining scrolls to match the first.

ATTACH THE ARMS

1. Wrap a 4-ft. piece of 3⁄16" round rod around a 3" pipe, as many times as possible.
2. Use bolt cutters to cut 120° arcs from the circles. These are the candle arms (B).
3. Lay a scroll on a flat work surface. Place the candle arm and support arm according to the scroll detail.
4. Weld the arms to the scroll. Using the first scroll as a pattern, place and weld the remaining candle and support arms (see bottom photo).

ASSEMBLE THE CHANDELIER

1. To make the rings (C), wrap a 2-ft. piece of 3⁄16" round rod around 1" pipe. Clamp the bent rod in a bench vise and saw through one side to form rings. Weld the ring ends together to complete.
2. On a large piece of cardboard or paper, draw a circle divided into six equal sections (60° between each line).
3. Lay out two scrolls back to back. Mark where the scrolls touch. Use one scroll as a pattern to mark the remaining scrolls.
4. Tack-weld a ring to the top mark of one scroll. Tack-weld the second ring to the lower mark on the same scroll.
5. Stand these pieces upright on one of the lines in the divided circle. Stand the opposing scroll up on the line and tack-weld the scroll to the upper and lower rings (see top photo, opposite page).
6. Weld the remaining scrolls to the rings. The

Make the second scroll bend around a 4" bending form.

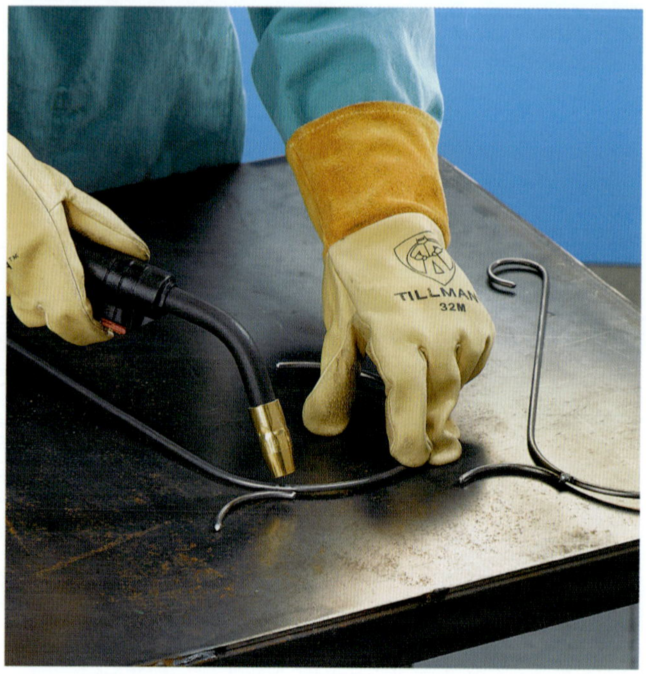

Weld the candle arms to the large end of the scrolls, even with the ring mark.

chandelier should be even and symmetrical. Adjust if necessary and complete the welds.

MAKE THE HANGER

1. Cut the crossbar (D) to length.
2. Weld the crossbar into the upper ring.
3. Cut the hanger (E) to length. Weld it upright to the centre point of the crossbar.
4. Clamp the rod for the hanging ring (F) to a ½" tube. Bend the rod around the tube. Mark the overlap point and cut. Weld the ends of the ring together.
5. Weld the hanging ring to the end of the hanger.
6. Attach a loop of string or wire to the hanging ring and hold up the chandelier. It should hang straight. If not, adjust the position of the hanging rod or ring.

ATTACH THE BOBECHES AND CANDLE CUPS

1. Drill four 3⁄32" holes around the perimeter of each bobeche.
2. Drill two 3⁄32" holes at the ends of the widest leaves in the acanthus.
3. Stand the chandelier upright on a level surface.
4. Place a bobeche (G) on a candle arm. Make sure it is level and weld in place. Repeat with the remaining bobeches.
5. Place a candle cup (H) in the centre of a bobeche. Weld in place. Repeat with the remaining candle cups.
6. Bend an acanthus leaf (I) around the outside of the lower scroll base. Weld in place (see photo, bottom right). Repeat with the remaining leaves.

FINISH THE CHANDELIER

1. Wire brush or sandblast the chandelier.
2. Finish as desired. The project as pictured is finished with white crackle over a gold base.
3. Attach the 1" teardrop crytals (J) to the bobeches. Attach the 3" hangdrop crystals (K) to the top ring. Attach the 3" teardrop prisms (L) to the acanthus leaves.
4. Attach a decorative chain, add candles, and hang.

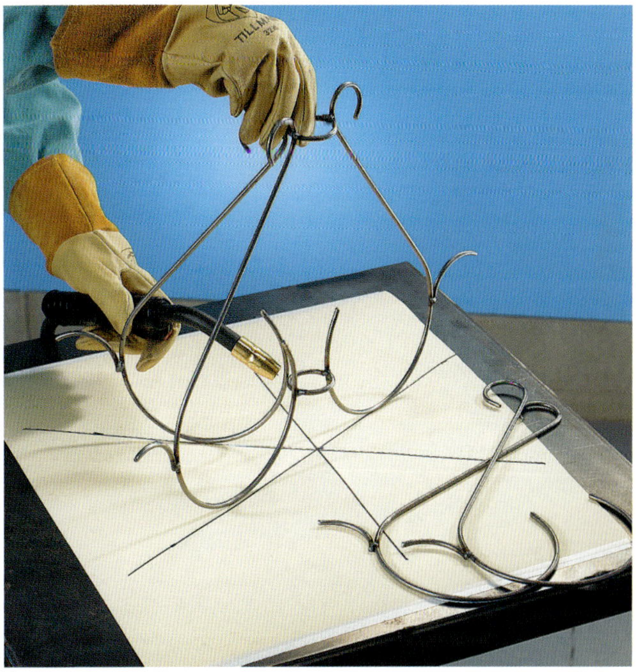

Using the pattern, weld the scrolls to the rings.

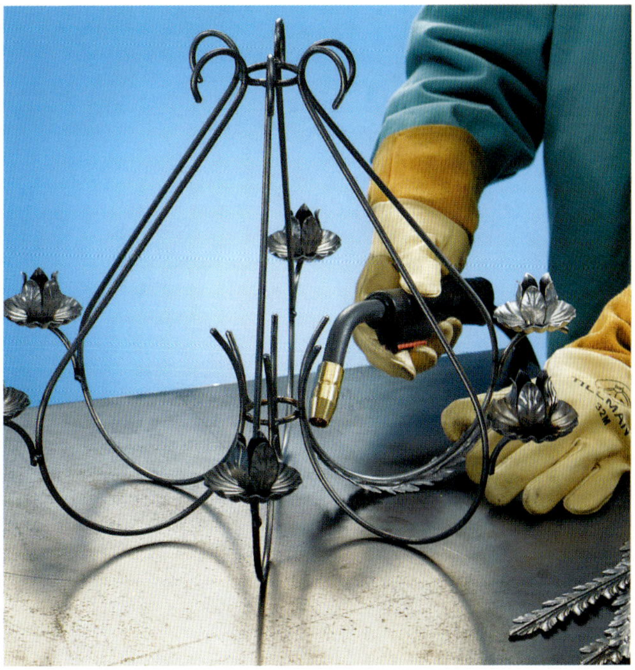

Bend the acanthus leaves to fit around the bottom curve of the scroll. Weld in place.

Note: This is a sharp-edged project and not recommended for households with small children.

Magazine Rack

Form follows function with this nifty M design. It's a magazine rack that's a snap to put together and perfect for keeping magazines organized and off the floor. You can use virtually any combination of sheet metal and tubing to make this rack. In this project, 16-gauge sheet metal and $\frac{3}{4}$ x 1$\frac{3}{4}$ rectangular tubing is used. You could also try it with round tubing, hammered tubing, pierced sheet metal, or expanded sheet metal. Make it to fit your favourite magazine, and it will be truly customized.

PART	NAME	DIMENSIONS	QUANTITY
A	Sides	16-gauge sheet metal 10 × 12"	2
B	Legs	16-gauge $\frac{3}{4}$ × 1$\frac{1}{2}$" rectangular tube × 10"	4

MATERIALS

- ⅛" sheet metal (2 ft. × 5 ft.)
- 16-gauge sheet metal (20 × 12" sheet)
- 16-gauge ¾ × 1½" rectangular tube (40")

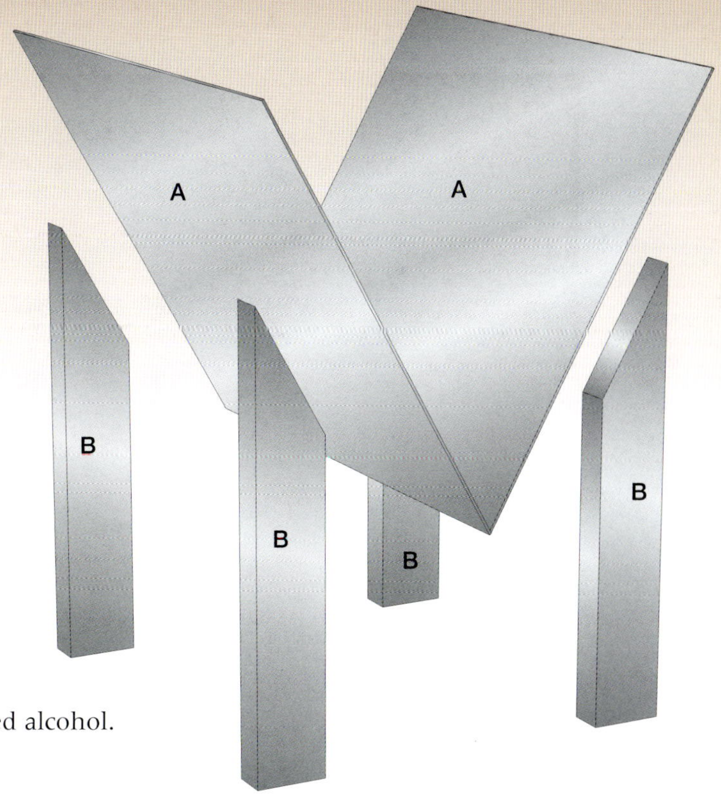

How to Build a Magazine Rack

Before welding, thoroughly clean all parts with denatured alcohol.

ASSEMBLE THE SIDES

1. Cut the sides (A) to size.
2. Remove slag and grind down any cutting imperfections.
3. Set up the sides in an upsidedown V. The V angle should be between 50° and 60°. Clamp the sides in place and tack-weld the sides together (see photo).
4. Weld the sides together with four 1" welds.

CUT THE LEGS

1. Cut the legs (B) to length.
2. To get the exact angle measurement for the angle at the top of the legs, trace the outside of the V on a piece of paper. Align a carpenter's square along the tops of the V, with one side of the V contacting the corner of the square. Mark the line for the leg (as though you are making an M). Repeat for the other side.
3. Flip the carpenter's square over and align it with one of the newly drawn lines. Align a leg in the corner of the square. Using a straightedge, mark the leg where it crosses the V. Repeat on the same side. Mark the remaining two legs using the other side of the pattern.
4. Cut the leg angles.

ASSEMBLE THE RACK

1. Place the V upside down. Place a leg about ½" in from the front or back end of the V. Use a try square to check that the leg is perpendicular and tack-weld in place.
2. Repeat Step 1 with the other three legs.
3. Turn the rack upright to check for leg alignment. Make adjustments, if necessary, and complete the welds.
4. Grind down welds and spatter. Wire brush the rack and wipe down with denatured alcohol before finishing.

Form a V with rack sides and clamp with magnetic clamps. Weld the seam.

Angled Metal Shelves

This shelf design is very versatile. The pattern can be altered infinitely—change the width, height, depth, and number of shelves to create a unit to fit in any space and display any item. Dress it up or down by using different materials. Consider using shelves with smooth tubing, a metallic finish, and glass (as we have done here), or use hammered tube, an antique finish, and weathered wood shelves for a rustic look.

MATERIALS

- $\frac{3}{4}$ x $1\frac{1}{2}$" rectangular tube ($24\frac{1}{2}$ feet)
- $\frac{1}{8}$ x $\frac{3}{4}$" flat bar ($2\frac{1}{2}$ feet)
- Tempered glass or wood (6 feet)

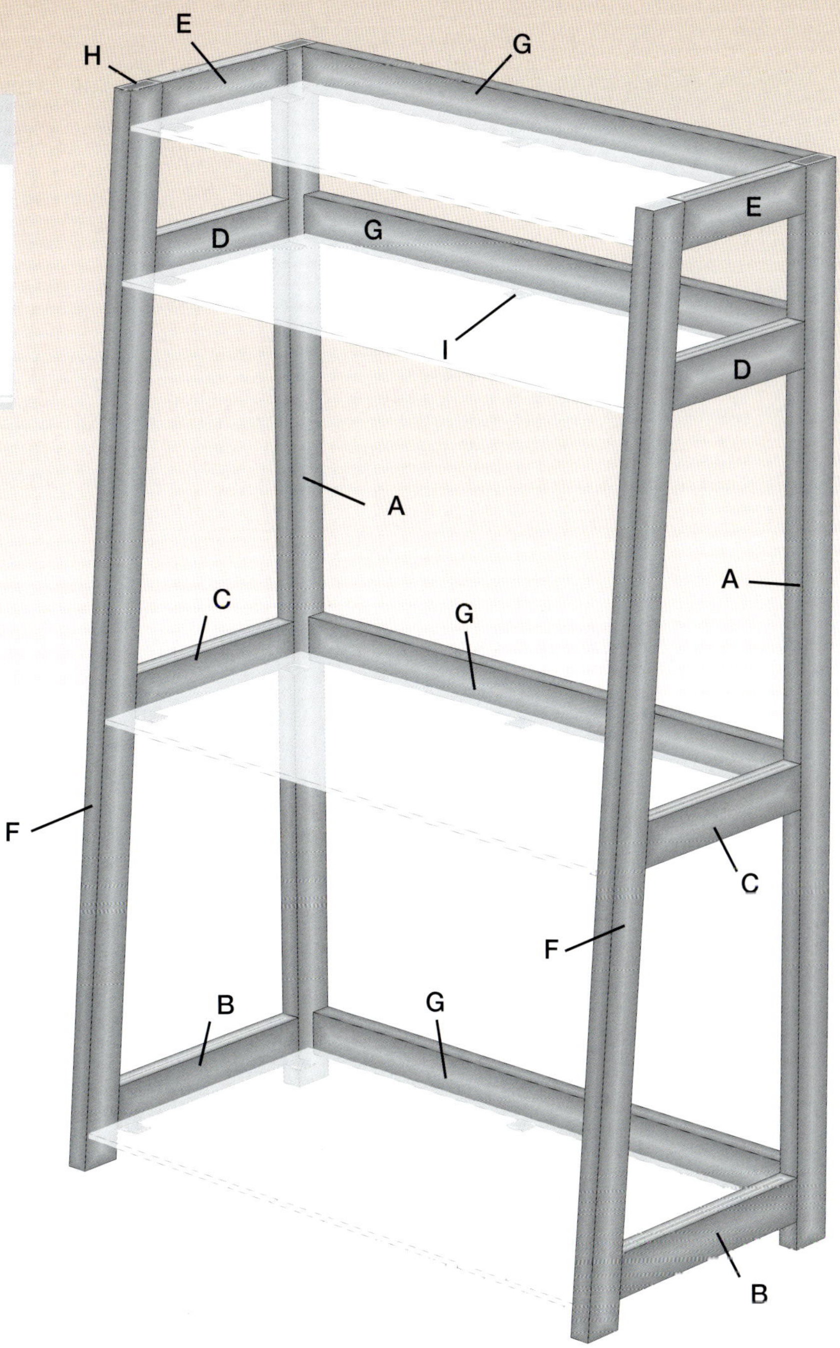

APART	NAME	DIMENSIONS	QUANTITY
A	Back legs	16-gauge $\frac{3}{4}$ x $1\frac{1}{2}$" rectangular tube x 36"	2
B	Bottom shelf sides	16-gauge $\frac{3}{4}$ x $1\frac{1}{2}$" rectangular tube x 9"	2
C	Middle shelf sides	16-gauge $\frac{3}{4}$ x $1\frac{1}{2}$" rectangular tube x $7\frac{3}{4}$"	2
D	Top shelf sides	16-gauge $\frac{3}{4}$ x $1\frac{1}{2}$" rectangular tube x $6\frac{1}{2}$"	2
E	Top sides	16-gauge $\frac{3}{4}$ x $1\frac{1}{2}$" rectangular tube x 6"	2
F	Front legs	16-gauge $\frac{3}{4}$ x $1\frac{1}{2}$" rectangular tube x $37\frac{1}{2}$"	2
G	Backs	16-gauge $\frac{3}{4}$ x $1\frac{1}{2}$" rectangular tube x 22"	4
H	End caps	$\frac{1}{8}$ x $\frac{3}{4}$" flat bar x $1\frac{1}{2}$"*	8
I	Shelf supports	$\frac{1}{8}$ x $\frac{3}{4}$" flat bar x $\frac{3}{4}$"	21
J	Shelves	Tempered glass*	3

* Cut to fit.

How to Build Angled Metal Shelves

Before welding, thoroughly clean all parts with denatured alcohol.

MAKE THE SIDES

1. Cut the back legs (A) to length.
2. Cut the shelf and top sides (B, C, D, E) to length with one end mitered at 83°.
3. Mark the back legs at 1", 7", and 15".
4. Align the flat end of the bottom, middle, and top shelf side pieces with the marks. Align the top side piece with the top of the back leg. Before welding, hold a straightedge against the angled side to check for alignment. Adjust if necessary. Tack-weld in place. Repeat with the other back leg and sides.
5. Align a front leg (F) with the side and back leg assembly. Using a carpenter's square held against the back leg, mark the top and bottom angled cuts for the front leg (see photo, below). Repeat with the other front leg.
6. Cut the first front leg to length along the marks.
7. Tack-weld the front leg to the side. Repeat with the second front leg.

To get the exact angle for cutting the front leg, align the tube with the side pieces and use a carpenter's square to mark a line even with the top of the top side.

After assembling the sides, weld the backs in place. Check for square both vertically and horizontally.

Weld the shelf supports to the bottom of the sides and backs.

ASSEMBLE THE SHELVES

1. Cut the backs (G) to size.
2. Stand a side unit on its back and line up a back piece with the top of the unit. Use a carpenter's square to check that the back is square to the side. Tack-weld in place (see photo, above left).
3. Align the second side unit with the back piece and tack-weld in place.
4. Repeat with the other three back pieces, aligning them with the top, middle, and bottom side pieces. Check for square and complete all welds.
5. Cut the end caps (H) to fit the tops and bottoms of the front and back legs. (The front pieces will need to be longer due to the angle.) Weld the caps to the leg ends. Grind down all the welds.

INSTALL SHELF SUPPORTS AND FINISH

1. Cut the shelf supports (I) to length.
2. Round the end of each with a bench grinder.
3. Weld two supports to the underside of each top, middle, and bottom shelf side piece. Weld three supports to each back piece (see photo, above right). Weld two supports 1" in from the sides and center the third on each back piece.
4. Sand, sandblast, or wire brush the unit. Finish as desired.
5. Measure the dimensions for each shelf and order tempered glass to fit, or cut wooden shelves.

WALL-MOUNTED SHELF

This wall-mounted shelf is perfect for displaying your decorative jars that hold cooking oils or spices. A single 24" square tile used for ceilings is cut to size at 24 × 6", which gives the appearance of four separate 6 × 6" tiles. A variety of tin tile sources are available on the Internet. You may also find ceiling tiles at salvage stores and antique stores—and they already have the antique character. The tiles don't need to be welding-quality steel; installing them with two-part epoxy is sufficient.

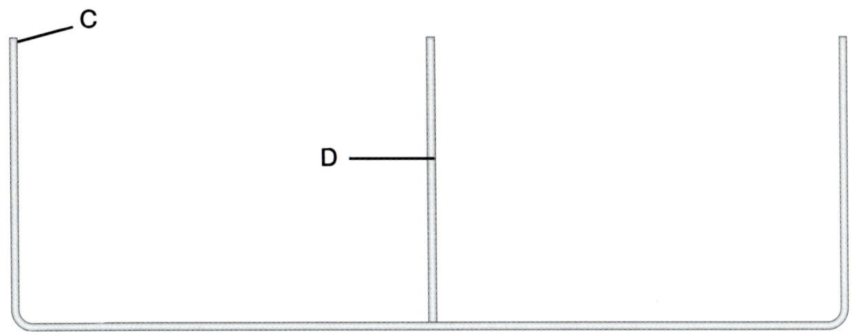

Bottom shelf

MATERIALS

- 1/4" round rod (18 1/2 feet)
- 1/8 x 1/2" flat bar (12 feet)
- 24" metal ceiling tile (1, M-BOSS #0613)
- 3/16" round rod (5 feet)

PART	NAME	DIMENSIONS	QUANTITY
A	Frame	1/4" round rod x 64"	1
B	Tile supports	1/4" round rod x 8"	3
C	Shelf frames	1/4" round rod x 36"	2
D	Shelf supports	1/4" round rod x 6"	1
E	Shelf cross pieces	1/8 x 1/2" flat bar x 24"	6
F	Top scrolls	1/4" round rod x 15"	2
G	Top circle	1/4" round rod x 12"	1
H	Side shelf scrolls	3/16" round rod x 9"	2
I	Front shelf scroll	3/16" round rod x 15"	2
J	Shelf circle	3/16" round rod x 10"	1
K	Tin tile	24" x 6"	1

How to Build a Wall-Mounted Shelf

Before welding, thoroughly clean all parts with denatured alcohol.

CREATE THE FRAME

1. Cut the frame (A) to length.
2. Mark the frame at 12", 19¾", 43½", and 52¼". Create a rectangle by making 90° bends at the marks. Weld the ends together.
3. Cut the tile supports (B) to length.
4. Weld the tile supports into the frame at 6" intervals (see photo, below).

CREATE THE SHELF

1. Cut the shelf frames (C) to length.
2. Mark each of the shelf frames at 6" in from each end. Make 90° bends at the marks to create the shelf frames.
3. Weld one shelf frame to the base of the frame at a 90° angle.
4. Cut the shelf supports (D) and cross pieces (E) to length.
5. Weld the first shelf support to the installed shelf frame at the midpoint. Weld the remaining two supports centered between an outside edge of the shelf frame and the centre shelf support.
6. Space the shelf cross pieces at ½" intervals across the supports. Weld in place.
7. Weld the second shelf frame to the frame 2" above the shelf at a 90° angle (see photo, opposite left).

Weld the tile supports to the frame at 6" intervals.

Weld the top shelf frame to the frame 2" above the shelf.

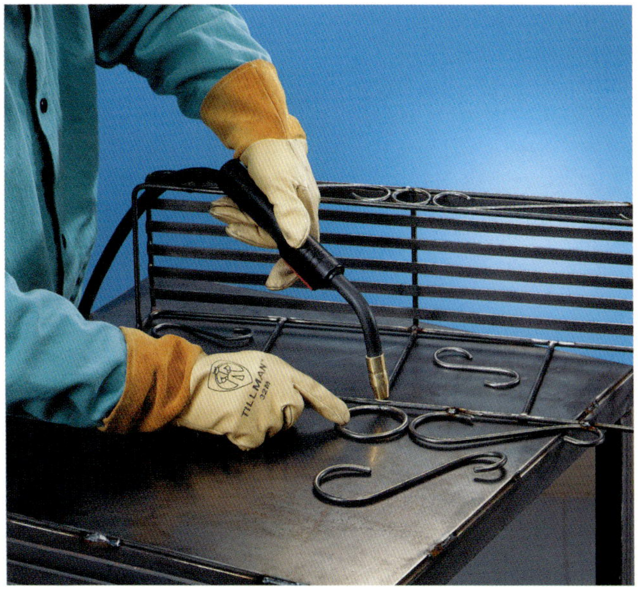

Weld the decorative scrolls and circles to the frames.

MAKE THE SCROLLS

1. Cut the top (F), side (H), and front (I) scrolls to length.
2. Clamp the top scroll rod to a 2" pipe. Bend the rod one full turn around the pipe. Clamp the other end around a 1" pipe and bend the rod one full turn around the pipe in the opposite direction from the first bend. Repeat with the second top scroll, making sure the scrolls match.
3. Clamp the end of a front shelf scroll to a 1" pipe. Bend the rod one full turn around the pipe. Clamp the other end to the pipe and bend the rod one full turn around the pipe in the opposite direction. Repeat with the second front scroll.
4. Clamp the end of a side scroll to a 1" pipe. Bend the rod one turn around the pipe. Clamp the other end to a 1" pipe and bend the rod one turn around the pipe in the opposite direction. Repeat with the second side scroll.
5. Bend the top circle (G) around a 2" pipe, overlapping the ends. Cut the overlap off and weld the circle ends together.
6. Bend the shelf circle (J) around a 1" pipe, overlapping the ends. Cut the overlap off and weld the circle ends together.
7. Place the shelf unit on its back and align the top scrolls and circle along the top. Weld at the contact points (see right photo, above).
8. Align the front scrolls and circle in between the shelf and the shelf support. Weld at the contact points. Repeat with each of the side scrolls.

FINISH THE SHELF

1. Cut the tile down to a 6 × 24" strip, or 6" squares, depending on the tile and pattern you have chosen.
2. Use two-part epoxy to glue the tiles to the frame.
3. Sand, wire brush, or sandblast the shelf.
4. Finish as desired.

ÉTAGÈRE

Étagère is a French term for a metal structure used to display items, or, at the garden store, plants. Étagères can be shockingly expensive, but this project is not only affordable, but it is much sturdier than many available in stores. The corner shelf that follows (on page 78) is created to match the style of this project.

This decorated shelf may be used inside or outside the home. Paint it or allow it to gently rust. The decorative elements are not structural, so you may change them to suit your desired level of fuss. The flat expanded sheet metal was chosen because it repeats the diamond pattern, but anything from metal to wood to tile can be used as shelving material. Check out the decorative iron suppliers listed on the internet for dozens of friezes and metal stampings that may be used instead of the diagonals and scrolls.

MATERIALS

- 16-gauge 1 × 1" square tube (23 feet)
- 16-gauge ½" flat expanded sheet metal (2 ft. × 3 ft.)
- ¼" round rod (31 feet)
- ⅛ × ½" flat bar (5 feet)
- 1½" balls (4, Triple S Steel #SF116F4)
- 1 × 1" × ⅛" angle iron (6 feet)

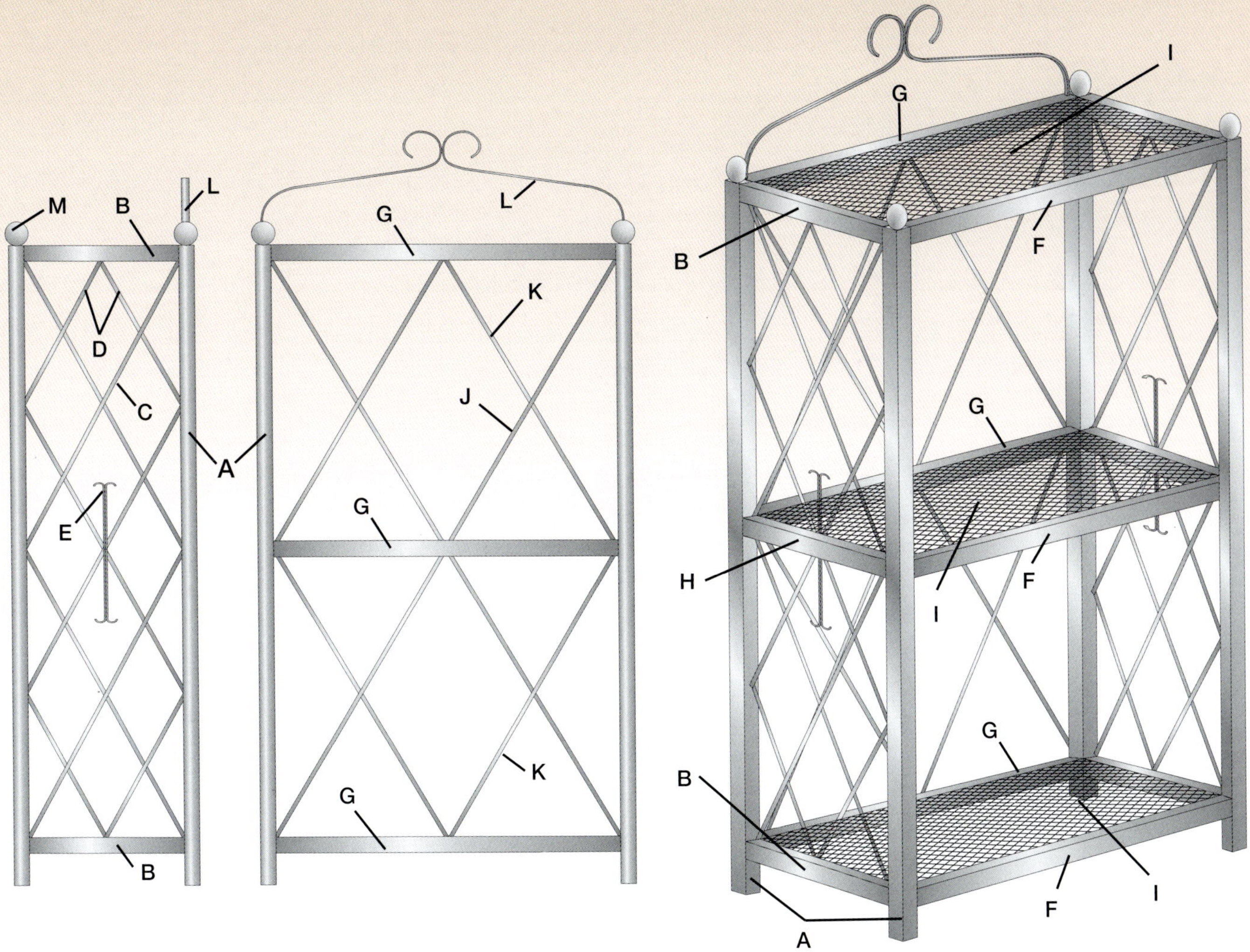

PART	NAME	DIMENSIONS	QUANTITY
A	Legs	16-gauge 1 × 1" square tube × 40"	4
B	Crossbars	16-gauge 1 × 1" square tube × 10	4
C	Long diagonals	¼" round rod × 21"*	12
D	Short diagonals	¼" round rod × 10"*	8
E	Side decorations	⅛ × ½" flat bar × 5¾"	8
F	Front supports	1 × 1" × square tube × 22"	3
G	Back supports	1 × 1" × ⅛" angle iron × 22"	3
H	Shelf supports	⅛ × ½" flat bar × 9"	2
I	Shelves	Expanded sheet metal 23" × 11"	3
J	Back long diagonals	¼" round rod × 43"	2
K	Back short diagonals	¼" round rod × 21"	4
L	Scrolls	⅛ × ½" flat bar × 24"	2
M	Balls	1½" diameter	4

*Approximate dimension, cut to fit.

How to Build an Étagère

Before welding, thoroughly clean all parts with denatured alcohol.

MAKE THE SIDES

1. Cut the legs (A) and crossbars (B) to length.
2. Mark each leg 2" from one end. This is the bottom of the leg.
3. On a flat work surface, lay out two legs and two crossbars. Align the bottom of one crossbar with the marks. Align the top of the other crossbar with the top of the legs. Clamp in place.
4. Check all corners for square. Tack-weld all corners. Recheck for square by measuring across the diagonals. If the two measurements are equal, the unit is square. If the measurements are not equal, make adjustments until they are. Complete the welds.
5. Repeat Steps 3 and 4 to make the second side panel.

CUT THE DECORATIVE SIDE DIAGONALS

1. Find the midpoint of the top and bottom crossbars and mark.
2. Find the midpoint of the front and back legs between the crossbars and mark.
3. Mark the points halfway between the midpoints and the crossbars. These are the quarterpoints.
4. Determine the lengths for the long diagonals (C) by measuring from a corner to the opposite midpoint and from an upper quarterpoint to a lower, opposite quarterpoint (see photo, below). (These measurements should be equal if the panel is square.) Cut the long diagonals slightly longer than this measurement.
5. Determine the lengths for the short diagonals (D) by measuring from a quarterpoint to the adjoining crossbar midpoint. Cut the short diagonals slightly longer than this measurement.
6. Hold the diagonals in place against the side panels and mark the necessary cutting angle. Cut at the marks.

Measure between a corner and the opposite midpoint to find the length for the long diagonals.

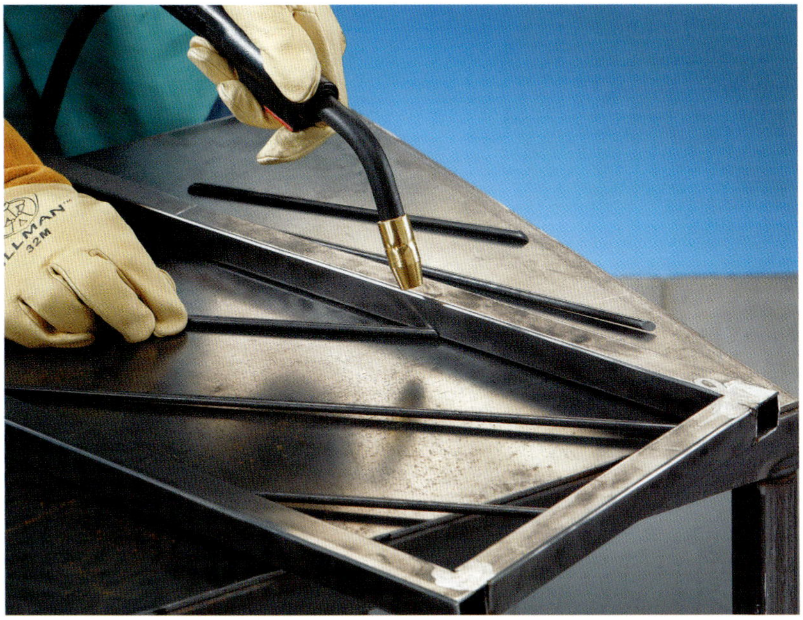

Weld the first layer of diagonals in place.

ASSEMBLE THE DECORATIVE SIDE DIAGONALS

1. With the side panel on a flat surface, lay the three long and two short diagonals that slant down from upper left to lower right in place. Weld to the frame (see photo, above).
2. Lay the three long and two short diagonals that slant from upper right to lower left in place on top of the other set of diagonals. Weld in place.
3. Cut the side decorations (E) to length. Round one end of each to a smooth semicircle, using a bench grinder.
4. Clamp the rounded end to a ½" pipe and bend the bar a ½ turn around the tube. Repeat with all the pieces.
5. Place two pieces back to back and weld together. Repeat with the other pieces.
6. Grind the flat ends of the decoration to a V.
7. Place one welded piece vertically upright at the middle of the diagonal pattern and weld in place. Place the second welded piece upside down at the middle and weld in place (see photo, top left on page 76).
8. Cut and assemble the diagonals for the second side panel.

ASSEMBLE THE ÉTAGÈRE

1. Cut the front supports (F) and back supports (G) to length.
2. The decorations on the side panels should be flush on one side and recessed on the other. The flush side is the outside. Place the two sides parallel to each other lying on their backs. Align the front supports with the top and bottom crossbars and centred over the midpoint. Check for square and tack-weld in place (see photo, top right on page 76).
3. Orient the top back support so the flat faces are to the top and front and aligned with the top crossbar. Tack-weld in place.
4. Orient the midpoint and bottom back supports with the flat faces to the top and back. Align with the front of the back leg. (This will allow the back panel decorations to be recessed).

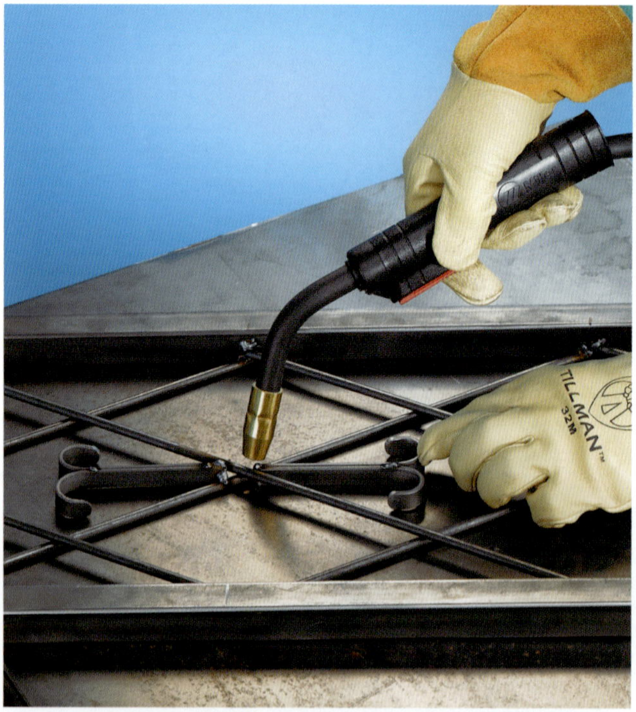

Weld the decorations to the middle X of the diagonals.

Tack-weld the front supports in place and check for square.

5. Cut the shelf supports (H) to length.
6. Weld the shelf supports flush with the top of the middle shelf frames at the ends. Bend the top shelf to fit inside the four supports (see photo, top left on page 77). Weld in place.
7. Cut the shelves (I) to size.
8. Bend the front of the middle shelf to fit behind the front support. The shelf lies on top of the shelf suport and back support. Weld in place.
9. Bend the front and sides of the bottom shelf to fit between the supports. The back lies on top of the back support. Weld in place.

MAKE THE BACK PANEL DECORATIONS

1. Measure the diagonal across the back of the shelves from corner to corner. Cut the back long diagonals (J) to this length.
2. Measure from the midpoint of the top back shelf support to the midpoint of the leg panel. Cut the short diagonals (K) to this length.
3. Place the left to right descending diagonals in place and weld. Place the right to left diagonals and weld.

MAKE THE DECORATIVE SCROLLS

1. Cut the scrolls (L) to length.
2. Round one end of each scroll to a smooth semicircle using a bench grinder.

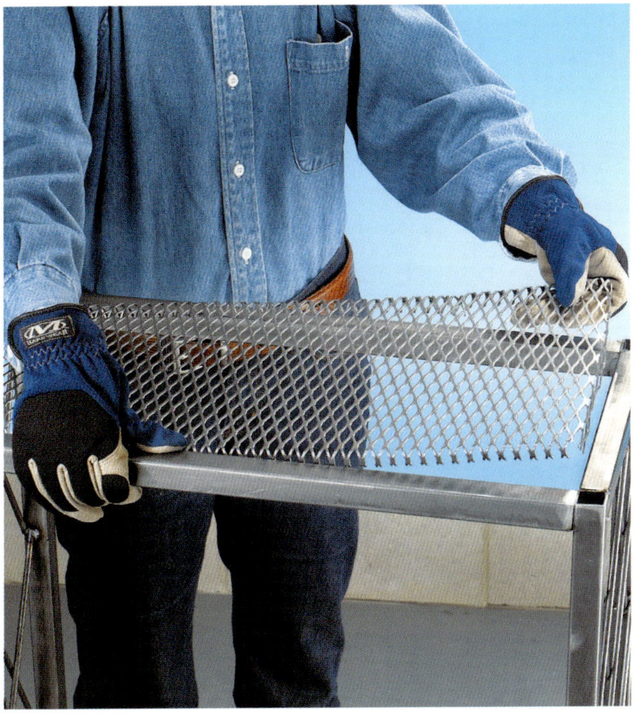

Bend the top shelf to fit inside the sides and supports.

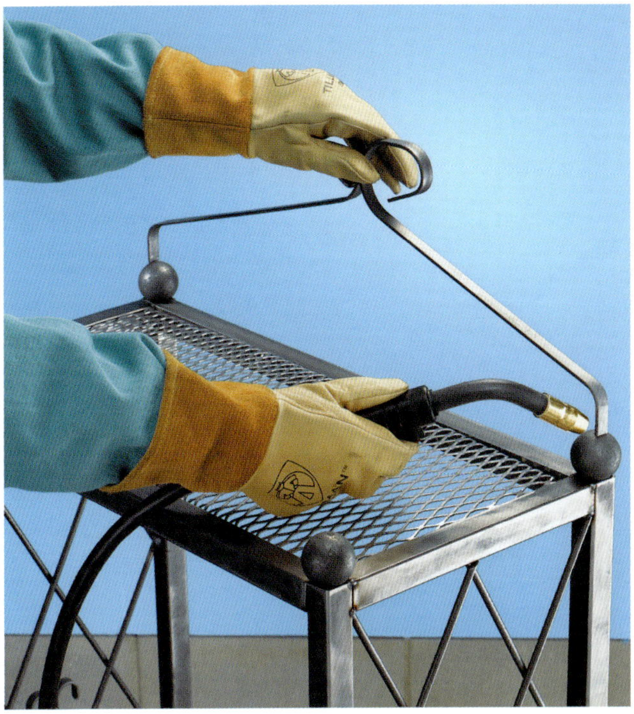

Weld the spheres to the tops of the legs and weld the scroll to the tops of the rear spheres.

3. Clamp the flat end to a 4" pipe and bend slightly past a 1/4 turn to create a rounded 90° angle. Repeat with the second scroll.
4. Cut a 1/8" notch in a 2" pipe.
5. Insert the rounded end of the scroll through both notches. Bend the scroll a 3/4 turn around the pipe. Repeat with the second scroll.
6. Weld the balls (M) into the tops of the legs (see Tip, below).
7. Align the two scrolls so they meet in the middle and are symmetrical. Weld at the contact points.
8. Weld the scrolls to the top of the rear balls (see photo, above right).
9. Sand, wire brush, or sandblast the shelf unit. Finish as desired.

TIP:

WELDING THICK MATERIAL TO THIN MATERIAL.

Welding solid spheres to 16-gauge material won't be successful without an extra step. The spheres will not weld easily because they absorb a great deal of heat before melting. Heating them first with a propane torch assures a good weld.

Corner Étagère

Why have an empty corner when it can display a beautiful shelf? Designed to match the étagère on page 72, this shelf unit is perfect for displaying plants or other decorative curios. You don't need to hide it in a corner—it can stand on its own in your backyard, or you can build two to create a semi-circle shelf to stand out along a wall.

The arcing shelf fronts look fancy but are actually fairly simple to execute. Face the front with a decorative frieze or metal stampings for a different look. The diagonals do not provide structural support, so you may personalize the sides in any way you choose.

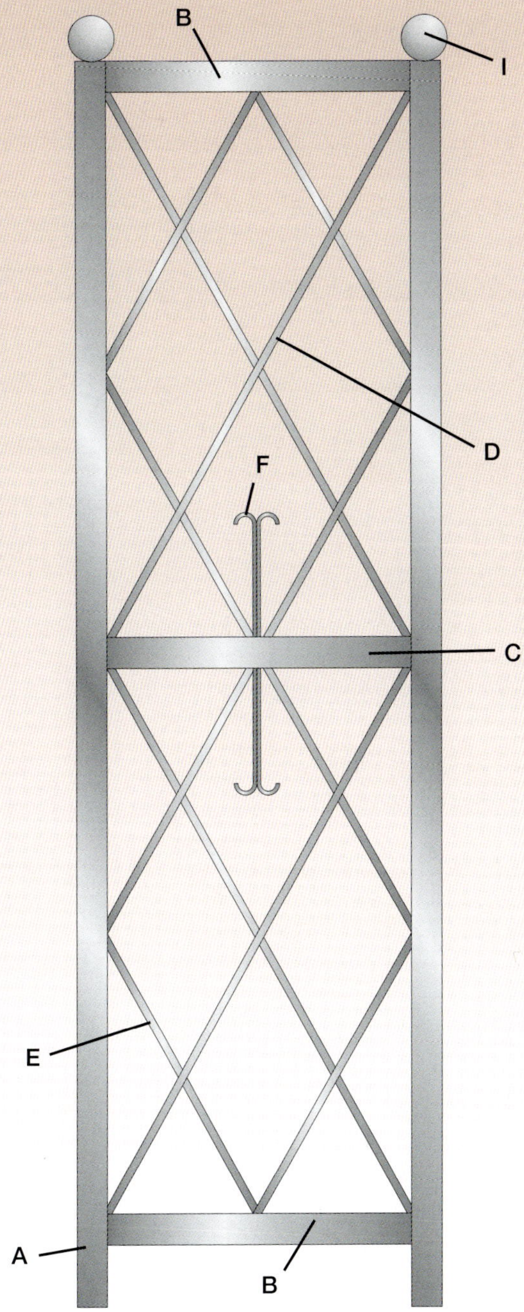

MATERIALS

- 16-gauge 1 × 1" square tube (10 feet)
- ¼" round rod (15½ feet)
- ⅛ × 1" flat bar (4½ feet)
- 16-gauge ½" flat expanded sheet metal (2 ft. × 2 ft.)
- 1½" balls (3, Triple S Steel #SF116F4)
- 1 × 1 × ⅛" angle iron (20")

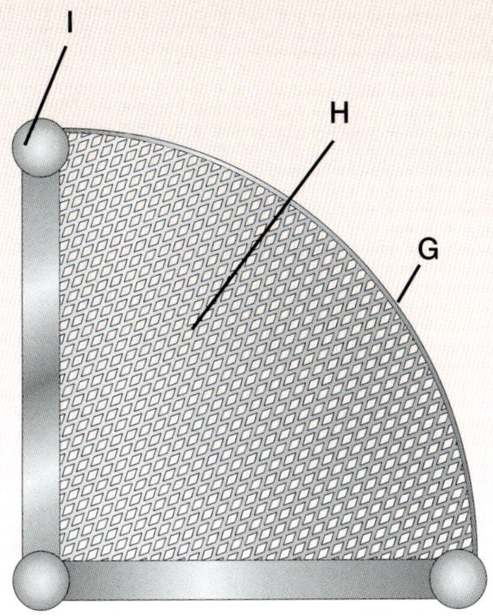

PART	NAME	DIMENSIONS	QUANTITY
A	Legs	16-gauge 1 × 1" square tube × 40"	3
B	Crossbars	16-gauge 1 × 1" angle iron × 10"	4
C	Middle crossbars	1 × 1 × ⅛" angle iron × 10"	2
D	Long diagonals	¼" round rod × 21"*	12
E	Short diagonals	¼" round rod × 10"*	8
F	Decorations	½ × ⅛" flat bar × 5¾"	8
G	Shelf fronts	⅛ × 1" flat bar × 18"	3
H	Shelves	16-gauge expanded sheet metal*	3
I	Balls	1½" dia.	3

* Cut to fit.

How to Build a Corner Étagère

Before welding, thoroughly clean all parts with denatured alcohol.

MAKE THE FRAME

1. Cut the legs (A) and crossbars (B) to length.
2. Measure 2" up from the ends of the legs and make a mark.
3. Align one crossbar in between and flush with the tops of two legs. Check for square and tack-weld in place. Align the bottom of a second crossbar with the end marks, check for square and tack-weld in place.
4. Measure across the diagonals of this unit to check for square. The measurements should be equal; if not, adjust until they are. Weld in place.
5. Repeat Steps 3 to 4, attaching the third leg and the crosspieces to the leg unit at right angles to form a triangular frame (see photo, below left).
6. Cut the middle crossbars (C) to length, mitreing one end at 45°. Centre the crossbars over the midpoints and even with the insides of the legs. Weld in place.

CUT THE DECORATIVE DIAGONALS

1. Find the midpoint of the top and bottom crossbars and mark.
2. Find the midpoint of the front and back legs between the crossbars and mark.
3. Mark the points halfway between the midpoints and the crossbars. These are the quarterpoints.
4. Determine the lengths for the long diagonals (D) by measuring from a corner to the opposite midpoint and from an upper quarterpoint to a lower, opposite quarterpoint. Cut the long diagonals to length. Place the diagonals and mark the angled cut necessary for an exact fit (see photo, below right).
5. Determine the lengths for the short diagonals (E) by measuring from a quarterpoint to the adjoining crossbar midpoint. Cut the short diagonals to length. Cut the long diagonals to length. Place the diagonals and mark the angled cut necessary for an exact fit (see photo, below right).

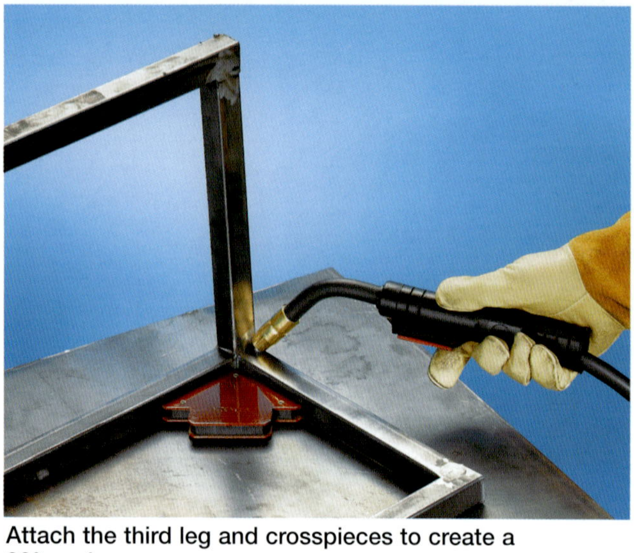

Attach the third leg and crosspieces to create a 90° angle.

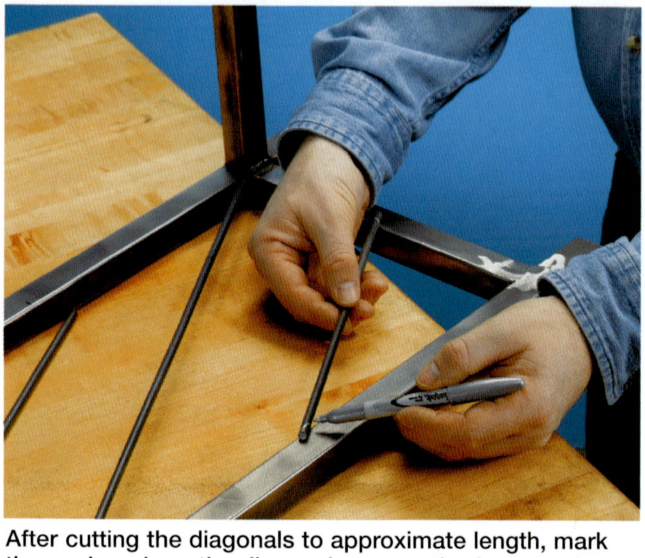

After cutting the diagonals to approximate length, mark the angles where the diagonal crosses the framework.

Before welding, thoroughly clean all parts with denatured alcohol.

MAKE THE FRAME

1. Cut the legs (A) and crossbars (B) to length.
2. Measure 2" up from the ends of the legs and make a mark.
3. Align one crossbar in between and flush with the tops of two legs. Check for square and tack-weld in place. Align the bottom of a second crossbar with the end marks, check for square and tack-weld in place.
4. Measure across the diagonals of this unit to check for square. The measurements should be equal; if not, adjust until they are. Weld in place.
5. Repeat Steps 3 to 4, attaching the third leg and the crosspieces to the leg unit at right angles to form a triangular frame (see photo, below left).
6. Cut the middle crossbars (C) to length, mitreing one end at 45°. Centre the crossbars over the midpoints and even with the insides of the legs. Weld in place.

CUT THE DECORATIVE DIAGONALS

1. Find the midpoint of the top and bottom crossbars and mark.
2. Find the midpoint of the front and back legs between the crossbars and mark.
3. Mark the points halfway between the midpoints and the crossbars. These are the quarterpoints.
4. Determine the lengths for the long diagonals (D) by measuring from a corner to the opposite midpoint and from an upper quarterpoint to a lower, opposite quarterpoint. Cut the long diagonals to length. Place the diagonals and mark the angled cut necessary for an exact fit (see photo, below right).
5. Determine the lengths for the short diagonals (E) by measuring from a quarterpoint to the adjoining crossbar midpoint. Cut the short diagonals to length. Cut the long diagonals to length. Place the diagonals and mark the angled cut necessary for an exact fit (see photo, below right).

ASSEMBLE THE DECORATIVE DIAGONALS

1. With the side panel on a flat surface, lay the three long and two short diago-

Weld the arched fronts to the sides, even with the crossbars.

Use a hand seamer and pliers to bend the expanded sheet metal to fit inside the top and bottom crossbars.

Window Box

Window boxes are a great way to increase your gardening area and create beautiful accents to your home. The box may be lined with a single liner or a 2 × 8 board can be placed upon the base crossbars to support individual pots. This is a basic box for a picture window, decorated with C-scrolls and finials. The design may be resized to be shorter and may be dressed up with fancier scrolls, finials, or decorative panels.

Check the Internet for suppliers of pre-punched bar channel, finials, and other decorative accents. The materials list is based on cuts made with a hacksaw or bandsaw. If you use a cut-off grinder, you will need to add additional material to compensate for the larger kerf. The box is heavy when filled with liner, dirt, and plants, so mount it securely in studs, using lag screws long enough to penetrate house sheathing and siding.

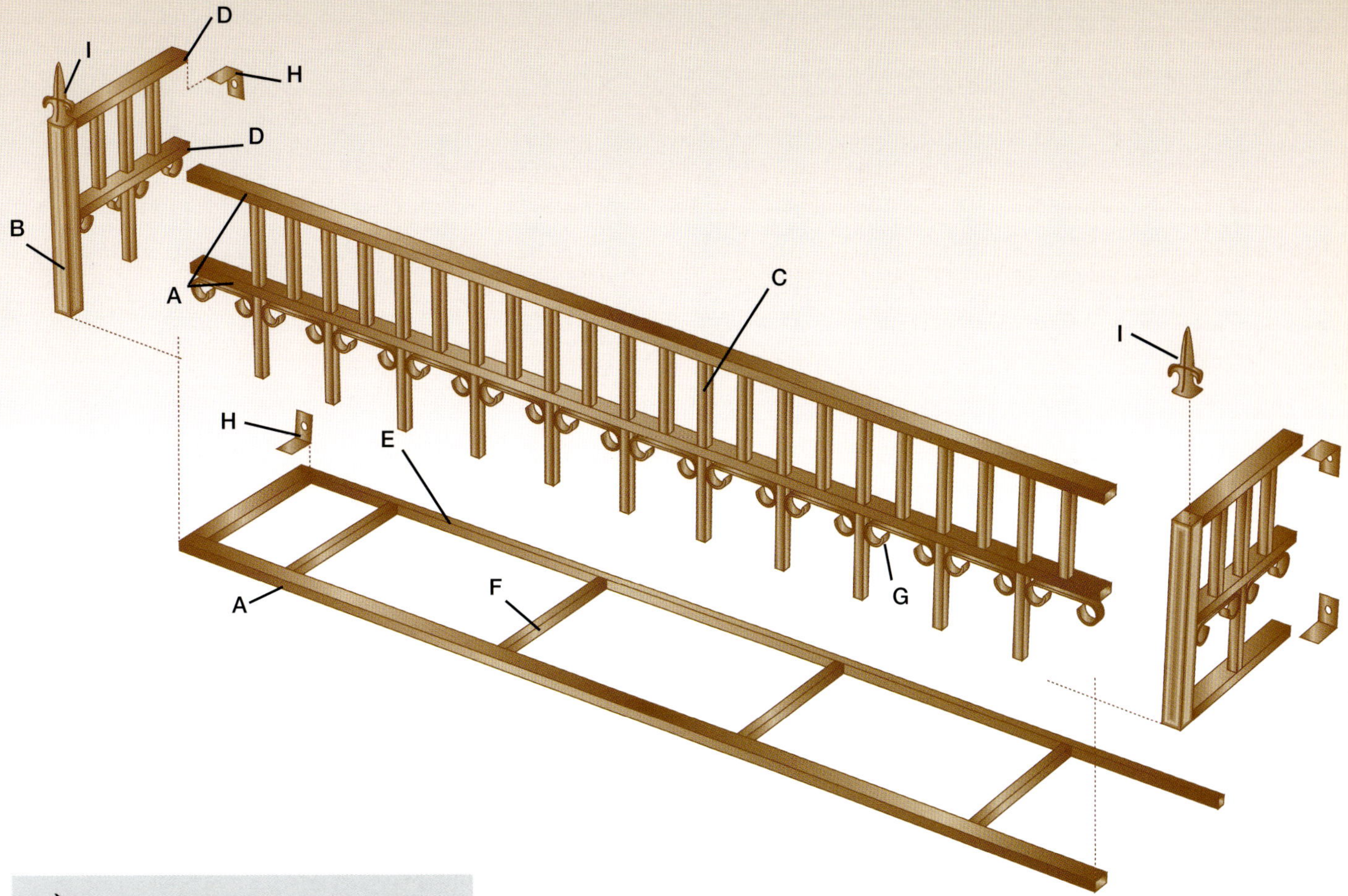

MATERIALS

- 1 × ½ × ⅛" channel (18 feet)
- 1" square tube (20")
- ½" square tube (16 feet)
- ½" square bar (8 feet)
- ⅛ × ½" flat bar (14½ feet)
- ⅛ × 1" flat bar (8")
- Finials (2, Architectural Iron #83/4)

PART	NAME	DIMENSIONS	QUANTITY
A	Front crossbars	1 × ½ × ⅛" channel × 52½"	3
B	End posts	16-gauge 1" square tube × 10"	2
C	Uprights	16-gauge ½" square tube × 4¼"	42
D	Side crossbars	1 × ½ × ⅛" channel × 8⅞"	6
E	Base	½" square bar × 54½"	1
F	Base crossbars	½" square bar × 9¾"	4
G	C-scrolls	⅛ × ½" flat bar × 10½"	16
H	Mounting brackets	⅛ × 1" flat bar × 2"	4
I	Finials		2

How to Build a Window Box

Before welding, thoroughly clean all parts with denatured alcohol.

ASSEMBLE THE FRONT PANEL

1. Cut the front crossbars and end posts (A and B) to length. Cut the uprights (C) to length.
2. On a flat surface, lay out the front of the window box. Align the bottom crossbar with the bottom of the end posts. Check for square and tack-weld in place.
3. Place two uprights between the bottom bar and the middle crossbar. Slide the middle crossbar up snug against the uprights. Check that the middle crossbar is square to the end posts and tack-weld in place (see photo, below).
4. Place two uprights between the middle and top crossbars. Slide the top crossbar snug against the uprights. Check that the top bar is square to the end posts and weld in place.
5. Verify that the front panel is square by measuring both diagonals. If they are equal, the panel is square. Once the panel is square, weld the joints between the crossbars and the end posts.
6. Place uprights centred every 4½" between the bottom and middle crossbars. Weld in place (see photo, below).
7. Place uprights centered every 2½" between the middle and top crossbars. Weld in place.

ASSEMBLE THE SIDE PANELS

1. Cut the side crossbars (D) to length.
2. Stand the front panel upright. Weld the bottom side crossbar in place. Using a right-angle magnetic clamp, clamp the middle crossbar in place. Check that the crossbar is square to the end post. Tack-weld in place (see top photo, opposite page).
3. Clamp the top side crossbar in place and weld.
4. Complete the welds to the end post and weld the uprights in place.
5. Assemble the other side panel by repeating Steps 2 to 4.

ATTACH THE BASE

1. Cut the base and base crossbars (E, F) to length.
2. Align the base with the back ends of the bottom side crossbars and tack-weld in place. Place the base crossbars at 6", 19", 33", and 46". Tack-weld in place. Complete the welds.

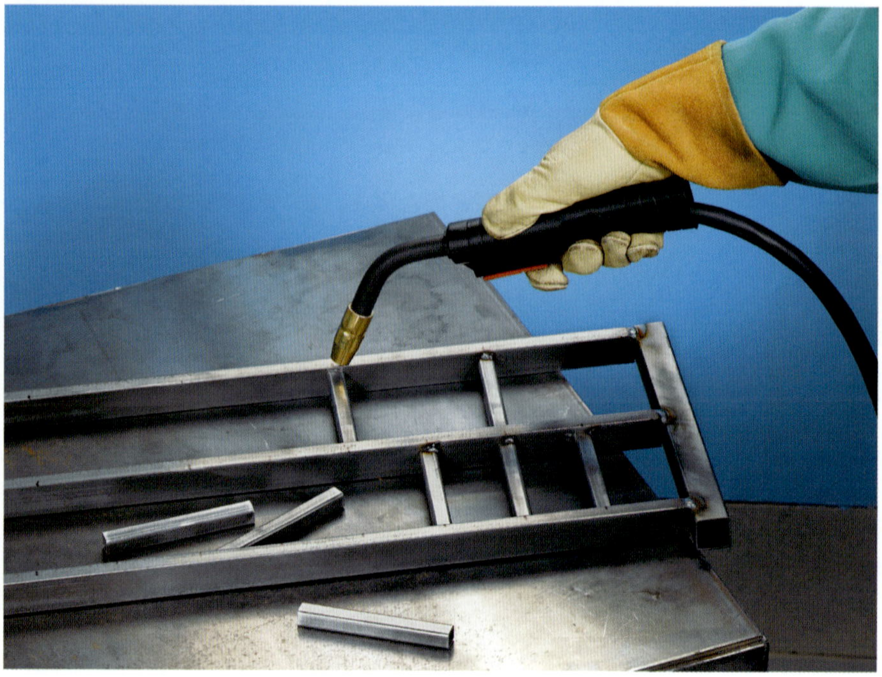

Weld the uprights into place between the crossbars.

MAKE THE C-SCROLLS

1. Cut the scroll blanks (G) to length. Round the corners of each end with a grinder. Clamp one end to a 1" pipe with a vise-style pliers. Bend the bar a 3/4 turn around the pipe. Clamp the other end of the bar to the pipe and bend a 3/4 turn around the pipe in the same direction to form a C-scroll (see bottom photo).
2. Place the C-scroll between two uprights to see if it fits. If not, adjust it by pulling the scrolls more open or pushing them more shut.
3. Continue bending and fitting C-scrolls until all have been made. Place the C-scrolls between uprights or end posts and the uprights. Align the flat edge of the C with the base of the middle crosspiece, leaving about a 1/8" gap. Don't place the scroll in the channel.
4. Weld the C-scrolls to the end posts and uprights.

FINISH THE WINDOW BOX

1. Cut the mounting brackets (H) to length. Drill a 3/16" hole, centered at 1/2", in each bracket.
2. Place the mounting brackets according to the diagram and weld in place.
3. Weld the finials (I) onto the end posts.
4. Finish the window box as desired.

MAKE A WINDOW BOX LINER

If you don't want to set up your window box with individual pots, you can make a window box liner out of sheet metal. If you want a heavy-duty, long-lasting liner, cut sides and a base of 16-gauge sheet metal and weld the parts to form a box to fit. Drill at least 6 drainage holes and paint. A 22-gauge liner, cut in one piece and bent with welds on the corners, is still a hefty liner. If you don't want to bother with welding or painting, cut and fold a liner from 24-gauge galvanized sheet metal with overlapping corners and rivet together.

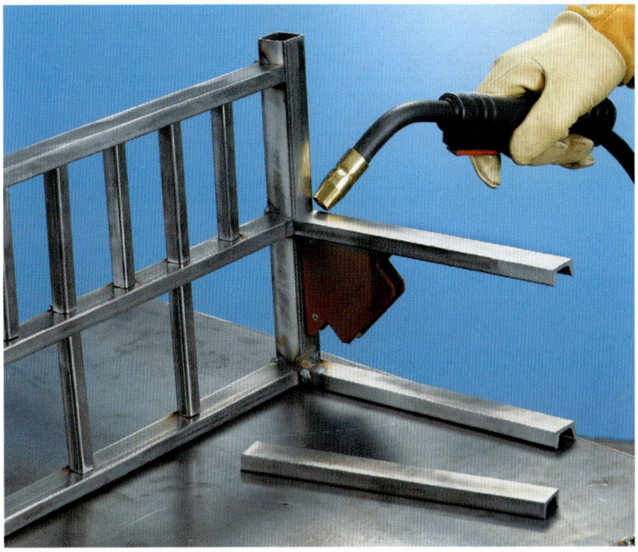

Weld the sides to the posts, even with the front crossbars.

Bend the C-scrolls using a 1" pipe bending form.

SQUARE FIRE PIT

All kids and most adults love having a fire in the back yard. Here's a fire pit that takes into account safety precautions, and it is easy to build. The deep box holds large chunks of wood, and the wide table lip minimizes scattering sparks. The footrests are great for kicking back by the fire, and they also help keep small hands away from the heat. If you want a spark screen, Smith & Hawken sells a clamshell screen on their website. This fire pit has been sized to use such a screen.

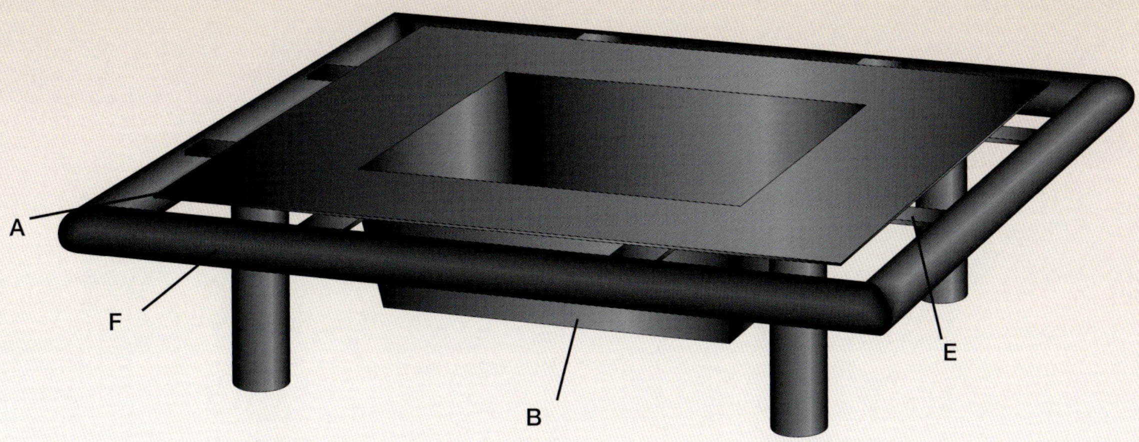

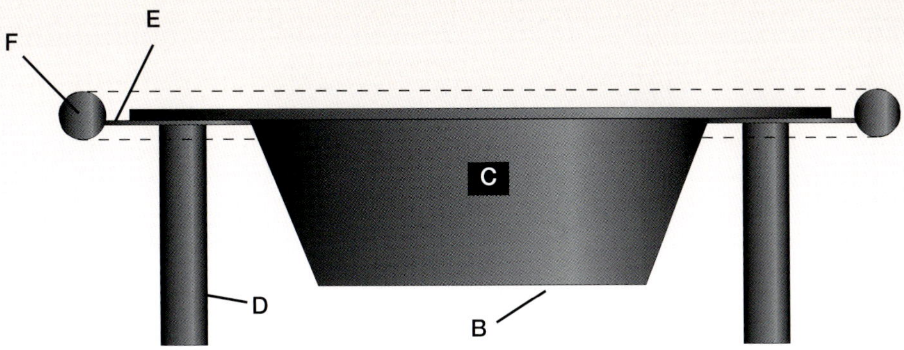

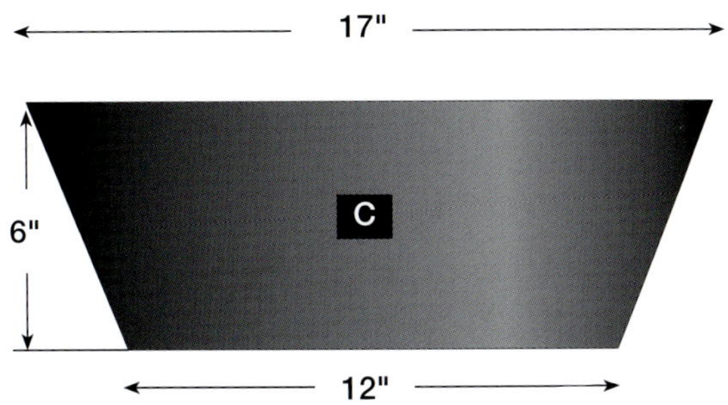

MATERIALS

- ⅛" sheet metal (30 × 30", 6 × 60½")
- ⅛ × ½ × 1" channel × 4 feet
- 16-gauge 2" round tube (15½ feet)
- Spark screen (Smith & Hawken #749622, optional)

PART	NAME	DIMENSIONS	QUANTITY
A	Top	⅛" sheet metal × 30 × 30"	1
B	Bottom	⅛" sheet metal × 12 × 12"	1
C	Sides	⅛" sheet metal × 12 × 17 × 6" (trapezoidal)	4
D	Legs	16-gauge 2" round tube × 9"	4
E	Arms	⅛ × ½" × 1" channel × 6"	8
F	Footrests	16-gauge 2" round tube × 36"	4

How to Build a Square Fire Pit

Before welding, clean all parts thoroughly with denatured alcohol.

MAKE THE TOP

1. Cut the top (A) to size.
2. Mark a straight line 6½" in from each side. This will create a centre square.
3. Using a plasma cutter or acetylene torch, cut the inside square out of the top.

MAKE THE BOX

1. Cut the bottom (B) to size by cutting down the scrap from the top. Mark in 5" from two sides of the scrap to form the 12" square (see photo, below). Cut along the lines.
2. On a 6 × 60½" piece of sheet metal, mark one long side at 17", 29", 46", and 58". Mark the other side at 21½", 14½", 31½", and 43½". Use a straightedge and marker or soapstone to draw lines from the corner to the 21½" mark, from the 14½" mark to the 17" mark and so on to create four trapezoids with the parallel sides being 17" and 12". Cut the sides (C) to size.
3. Tack-weld a side to the bottom. Tack-weld an adjacent side to the bottom. Bend the sides so their seam aligns, if necessary, and tack-weld. Continue with the other sides (see left photo, opposite page).
4. Turn the box over and weld all the seams.
5. Place the box over the cutout in the table and tack-weld in place.
6. Complete all the welds.

On the scrap piece cut from the top, mark 5" in from two edges to create a 12" square.

Tack-weld the sides to the base from the inside. Then turn the pit over and weld all the seams.

Creating a jig using a piece of channel iron and plywood makes cutting the 45° angles easier.

MAKE THE LEGS

1. Cut the legs (D) to length.
2. Place the legs 2" from each corner of the box. Weld in place.

MAKE THE FOOTREST

1. Cut the footrests (F) to length, mitreing each end at 45°. Make sure the mitres are perfectly aligned. Use a clamping jig to prevent rolling (see photo, above right).
2. Lay out the footrests to form a square. Tack-weld the corners.
3. Turn the table and fire box upside down on top of 1" spacers. Place the footrest around the top. Align the footrest evenly with the table edges.
4. Cut the arms (E) to length.
5. Place the arms so they touch the footrest and are aligned with the box edges.
6. Tack-weld the arms to the footrest. Tack-weld the arms to the table underside. Make sure the footrest is still aligned with the top.
7. Complete all the welds for the arms and footrests.

FINISH THE PROJECT

1. Grind down all welds.
2. Wire brush and clean fire pit.
3. Finish with Rustoleum High Heat spray enamel.

LAUNDRY-TUB PLANTER

Laundry tubs, galvanized or enameled, have always been popular as planters. But because they're all about the same height, a collection of tubs generally doesn't offer much visual variety. Add height to your garden with this frame that holds a laundry tub securely about 2 feet off the ground.

The laundry tub used in this project is moderately sized at 10 gallons. The 3⁄8" rod is quite substantial, so you can certainly use a 16-gallon tub, or even a half barrel. Make smaller versions with 1⁄4" rod for buckets or pots. The basic methods are the same, whether the tub is oval or round, short or tall, big or small.

MATERIALS

- 3⁄8" round bar (30 feet)
- 1⁄8 × 1" flat bar (9 feet)
- 10.5 gal. laundry tub (1, Main St. Supply)
- 1⁄2" plywood (4 × 4 sheet)
- 2 × 4 scraps
- Wood screws
- 3⁄16" round bar (10 feet)

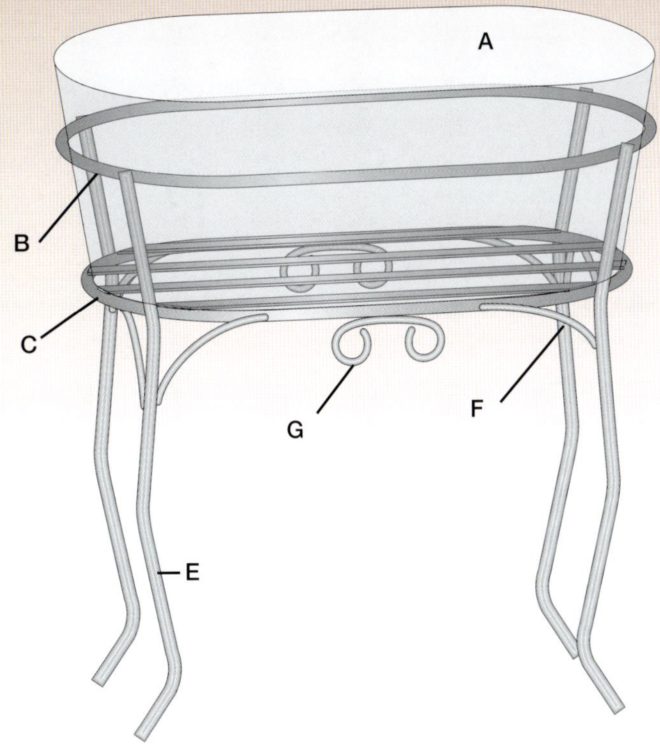

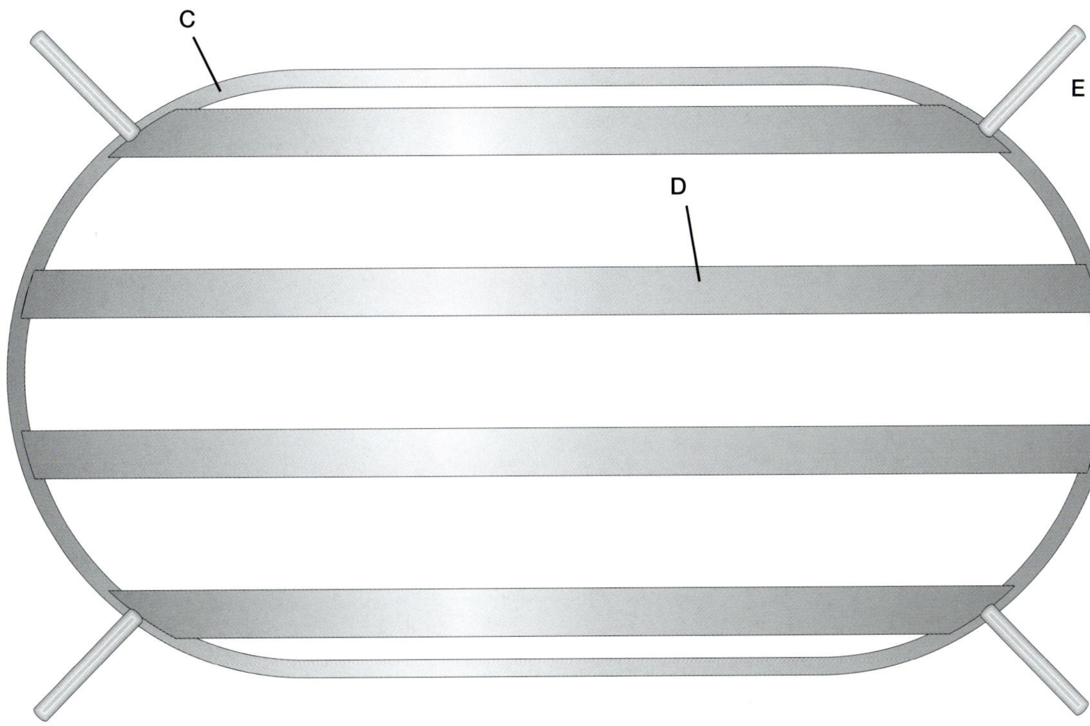

PART	NAME	DIMENSIONS	QUANTITY
A	Tub	10½ gallon	1
B	Tub support	3⁄8" round bar × 60"*	1
C	Base	3⁄8" round bar × 56"*	1
D	Crossbars	1⁄8 × 1" flat bar × 27"*	4
E	Legs	3⁄8" round bar × 25"	4
F	Leg braces	3⁄16" round bar × 10"	8
G	C-scroll	3⁄16" round bar × 15"	2

* Approximate dimensions, cut to fit.

How to Build a Laundry-Tub Planter

Before welding, thoroughly clean all parts with denatured alcohol.

MAKE THE BASE

1. Place the tub (A) upside down on a piece of plywood. Trace the outline of the tub. Turn the tub right-side up and centre it in the outline. Trace around the base of the tub and remove the tub. Create a third line halfway between the two lines. This is the pattern for the tub support.
2. Using a jigsaw, cut out the pattern for the tub support.
3. Attach the tub support pattern to a larger sheet of plywood, using screws. Place the 3/8" rod for the tub support (B) against a long side of the oval. Screw a wood block against the rod to hold it in place. Bend the rod around the pattern (see photo, below). Mark the rod for cutting where it overlaps itself.
4. Cut the rod and weld the ends together.
5. Remove the pattern from the backing board. Use a jigsaw to cut out the smaller oval pattern for the base. Attach the smaller oval pattern to the backer board. Create the base (C) following Steps 3 and 4 above.
6. Cut the crossbars (D) to fit on the base according to the diagram. Space the crossbars across the base at equal intervals and weld into place from the underside.
7. Grind or cut the overhanging ends of the crossbars so they match the oval base.

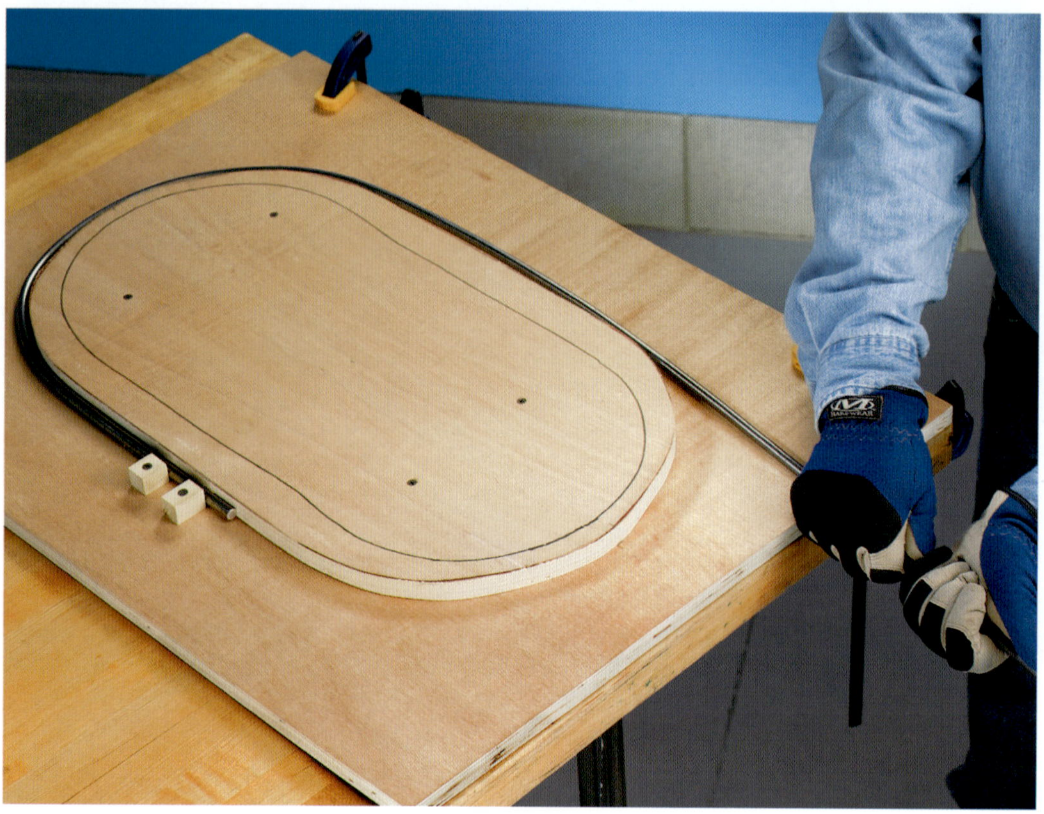

Bend the tub support around the jig.

MAKE THE LEGS

1. Cut the legs (E) to length.
2. Turn the tub upside down. Slide the tub support over the tub and place the base on the tub bottom. Hold a leg against the support and base to determine placement. Mark the leg where the base hits it. Mark the other three legs according to the first leg (see photo, top right).
3. Clamp a leg in a bench vise. Align the mark with the top of the vise. Bend the leg 110°. Repeat with the other three legs, using the first as a pattern.
4. Clamp a leg in the bench vise about 7" down from the first bend. Bend the leg the opposite direction about 10°. Repeat with the remaining legs.
5. Clamp the leg into the vise again, with the lower 2" of the leg protruding above the vise. Using a ½" pipe slid over the bar, bend the bar about 35°. Repeat with the remaining legs.

With the tub upside down, rest the tub support and base on the tub. Mark the leg blanks where they cross the base.

ATTACH THE LEGS

1. Place the tub upside down. Slide the tub support over the tub and place the base against the bottom of the tub.
2. Tack-weld a leg to the tub support and base (see bottom photo). Repeat with the other three legs. Remove the tub. Turn the assembly upright and make sure it is level and the legs are vertical. Adjust, if necessary, and complete the welds.
3. Using a 4½" bending form, bend the rod for the leg braces (F).
4. Place a leg brace so it contacts the leg about 5" down and contacts the base about 4" from the side of the leg. Mark the brace and cut it to fit.
5. Grind the leg end of the brace to a taper and weld in place. Repeat with the remaining leg braces.
6. Cut the C-scrolls (G) to length. Clamp one end to a 2" pipe and bend the rod a full turn around the pipe. Clamp the other end to the pipe and bend the rod one full turn in the same direction. Repeat to form the second C-scroll.
7. Centre the C-scrolls under the long sides of the base and weld in place.
8. Sand, wire brush, or sandblast the planter. Finish as desired.

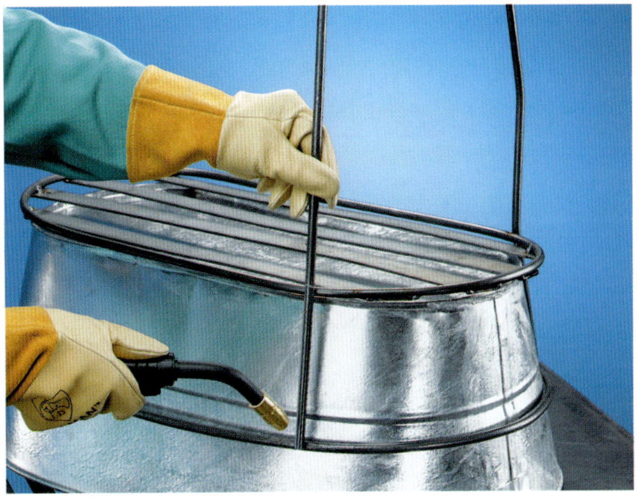

Tack-weld the legs in place, then remove the tub and finish the welds.

Cathedral Arbor

This arbor is a beautiful stand-alone piece, but it is also a brilliant addition to the Cathedral Arch with Gate (page 98). Either way it is an impressive addition to your yard. Mount it against a wall or fence, or use it as a panel within a fence. Better yet, make an entire fence of cathedral arches! To do so, screw mount the panels to 4 × 4 wood posts, or weld the panels to 3 × 3 steel posts.

You may want to cap off your arbor with a finial or decorate the panels with permanent trailing vines for the off-season. Check the Internet for finial, frieze, and stamped metal sources. Make sure to order parts that can be welded. Cast iron cannot be easily welded to the steel arbor parts.

MATERIALS

- 16-gauge 1 × 1" square tube (23 feet)
- 16-gauge ½ × ½" square tube (18 feet)
- ¾" round rod (6 feet)
- ⅛ × ½ × ½" angle iron (4")
- ¼" round rod (18 feet)

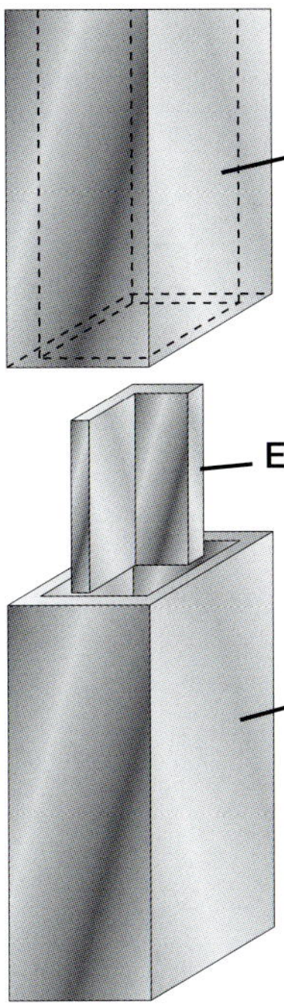

Sleeve detail

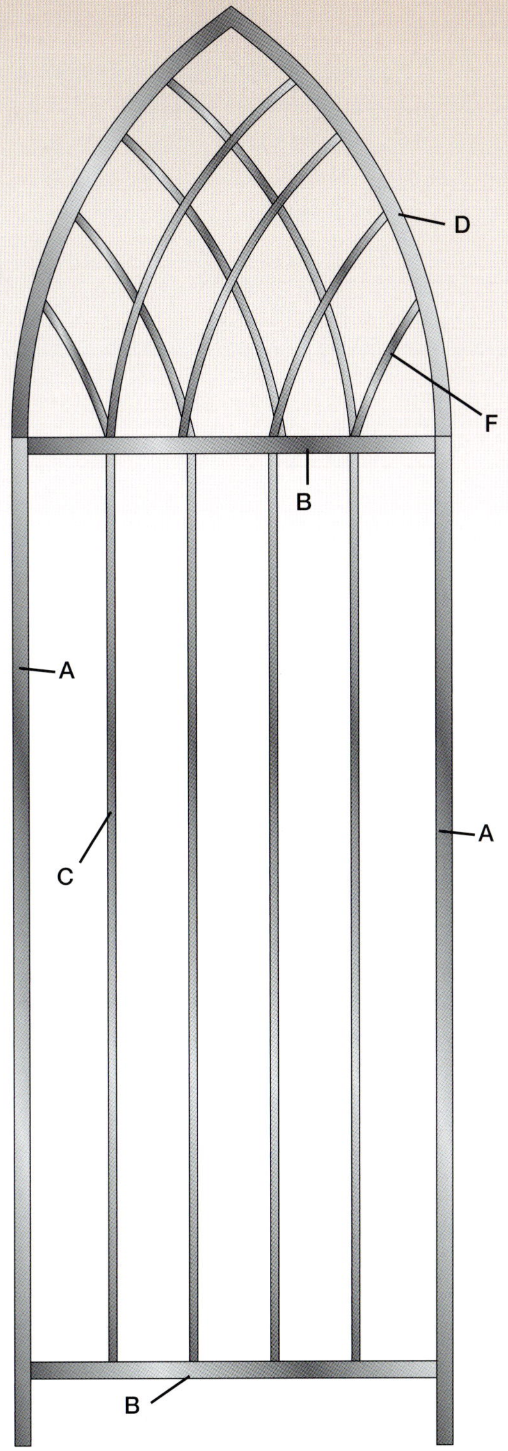

PART	NAME	DIMENSIONS	QUANTITY
A	Legs	16-gauge 1 × 1" square tube × 60"	2
B	Crossbars	16-gauge 1 × 1" square tube × 25"	2
C	Verticals	16-gauge ½ × ½" square tube × 54"	4
D	Main arch	16-gauge 1 × 1" square tube × 51"*	2
E	Sleeves	⅛ × ½ × ½" angle iron × 2"	2
F	Decorative arches	¼" round rod × varied*	8
G	Mounting stakes	¾" round rod × 36"	2

* Approximate dimensions, cut to fit.

How to Build a Cathedral Arbor

Before welding, clean all parts thoroughly with denatured alcohol.

Make the Panel

1. Cut the legs (A) and crossbars (B) to length.
2. Lay out the crossbars between the legs. Align the top crossbar with the top of the legs. Place the lower crossbar 4" from the bottom of the legs.
3. Check for square, clamp in place, and tack-weld together.
4. Measure across the diagonals to check for square. If the diagonals are not equal, adjust until they are. Complete the welds.
5. Cut the verticals (C) to length.
6. Mark the crossbars at 5", 10", 15", and 20". Centre the verticals at the marks, check for square, and weld in place.

Bend the Main Arches

1. Cut a 28" radius semicircle from ½" plywood. Cut the semicircle in half.
2. Stack the quarter circles and screw them onto a 3 × 3 sheet of plywood. Screw 2 × 4 stops along the bottom.
3. Clamp this bending jig to a stable work surface. Slide an arch piece (D) between the stops so it extends 2" below the bottom of the semicircle. Bend the tube around the curve (see top photo, opposite page). Bend the second arch in the same manner.

Finish the Main Arches

1. Remove the quarter circles from the bending jig. From the right angles of the quarter circles, measure in 17½" along one flat side. At this point, draw a line perpendicular to the side. Cut along the line. Repeat with the second quarter circle.
2. Mount these two arcs at the top of a 4 × 8 sheet of plywood, abutting them together on the new cuts to create a template for the arch.
3. Place one arch into the left side of the jig. Mark a vertical line on the arch to match the joint of the two wood arcs (see bottom photo, opposite page). Cut the arch along the line.
4. Place the other arch into the right side of the jig. Mark the centreline and cut.
5. Place both arches back into the jig and weld together at the peak.
6. Cut the sleeves (E) to length. Slide a sleeve 1" into each end of the arch. Slide the top of the panel over the sleeves. Weld the arch to the legs.

Make the Decorative Arches

1. Attach a stop block ½" from the base of the arch jig. Bend a decorative arch piece (F) around the jig to make a curve. Continue bending curves as needed.
2. At the 5" mark on the top crossbar, center one end of the arch piece. Align the arch parallel to the main arch. Mark the arch where it crosses the main arch (see bottom photo, opposite page). Cut on this line. At both ends, tack-weld in place.
3. Repeat Step 2 at the 10", 15", and 20" marks.

4. Repeat the process of placing, cutting, and welding arches for arches curving in the opposite direction. Finish all welds.
5. To prevent rattling, tack-weld the arches to each other where they cross.

FINISH THE ARBOR

1. Wire brush or sandblast the arbor. Finish as desired.
2. Pound the mounting stakes (G) 2 feet into the ground, 26" apart. Slide the legs over the mounting stakes.
3. Using wire, secure the top or sides of the arbor to a wall or fence.

Bend the arch around the jig. Insert a ½" black pipe into the tube end to create more leverage.

Place an arch in the second jig and mark where the arc crosses the vertical line between the two half circles.

After bending the decorative arches, mark where they cross the crossbar and main arches.

Cathedral Arch with Gate

What a grand entryway this arch and gate provides! Unlike many manufactured archways, this one stands a full 8 feet tall, allowing easy passage underneath and plenty of room for trailing foliage. It is proportioned to fit over a 42" walkway. The arching pattern is beautiful and fairly easy to create. When paired with the matching cathedral arbor (page 94), this project will really add class to your yard or garden.

Materials

- 16-gauge ½ × ½" square tube (48½ feet)
- 16-gauge 1 × 1" square tube (70 feet)
- ⅛ × ½ × ½" angle iron (8")
- ¼" round rod (48 feet)
- ¾" round tube (8 feet)
- 2" weldable barrel hinges (2 pair, Decorative Iron #14.1120)
- Gate latch (1, Decorative Iron #14.2012)
- ½" plywood (2, 4 × 8) sheets

Side view

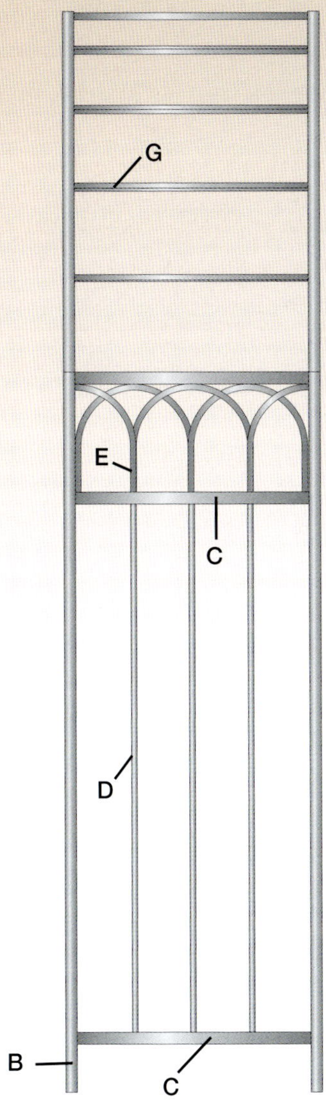

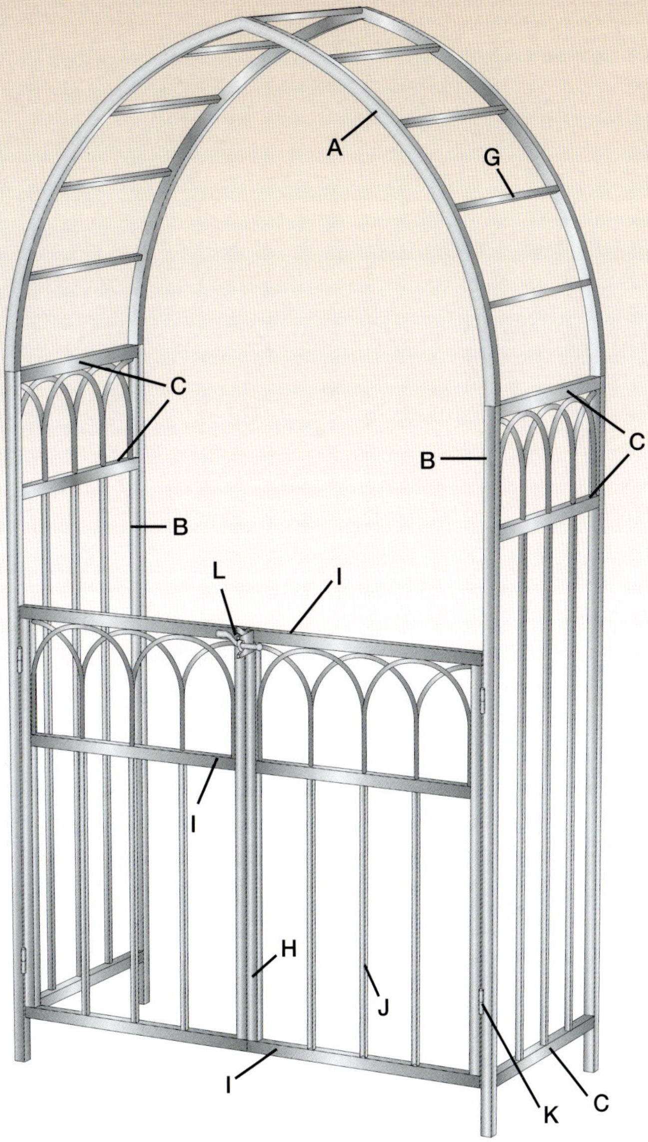

Leg arch detail

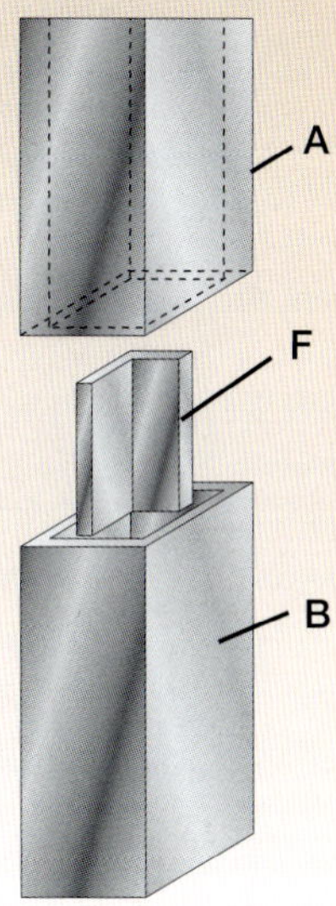

PART	NAME	DIMENSIONS	QUANTITY
A	Main arch	16-gauge 1 × 1" square tube × 51"*	4
B	Legs	16-gauge 1 × 1" square tube × 60"	4
C	Crossbars	16-gauge 1 × 1" square tube × 20"	6
D	Decorative vertical	16-gauge ½ × ½" square tube × 44"	6
E	Decorative arch	¼" round rod × 36"*	16
F	Sleeves	⅛ × ½ × ½" angle iron × 2"	2
G	Arch crossbars	16-gauge ½ × ½" square tube × 20"	9
H	Gate uprights	16-gauge × 1 × 1" square tube × 34"	4
I	Gate crossbars	16-gauge 1 × 1" square tube × $22\frac{3}{8}$"	6
J	Gate verticals	16-gauge ½ × ½" square tube × 23"	6
K	Barrel hinges	3"	4
L	Latch		1
M	Mounting stakes	¾" round tube × 24"	4

* Approximate dimensions, cut to fit.

How to Build a Cathedral Arch with Gate

Before welding, clean all parts thoroughly with denatured alcohol.

MAKE THE MAIN ARCHES

1. Cut a 28" radius semicircle from ½" plywood. Cut the semicircle in half.
2. Stack the quarter circles and screw them onto a 3 × 3 sheet of plywood. Screw 2 × 4 stops along the bottom.
3. Clamp this bending jig to a stable work surface. Slide an arch piece (A) between the stops, so it extends 4" below the bottom of the semicircle. Bend the tube around the curve (see top photo, page 97). Bend the remaining arches.

MAKE THE SIDE PANELS

1. Cut the legs (B) and crossbars (C) to length.
2. Lay out two legs and three crossbars on a flat surface. Align the top crossbar flush with the top of the legs and the base of the bottom crossbar 4" from the bottom of the legs (see photo, below). Align the top of the third crossbar 10" down from the top of the legs. Check for square, clamp in place, and tack-weld. Repeat to form the second side panel.
3. Before cutting the decorative verticals (D), measure between the bottom and middle crossbars for an exact length. Cut the decorative verticals to length. Mark all three crossbars at 5", 10", and 15".
4. Centre the verticals at the marks. Check for square and weld in place. Finish all welds.

Weld the crossbars to the legs.

CREATE THE DECORATIVE ARCHES

1. Make a bending jig by attaching a 9" diameter half circle and 10" long squares to a 15 × 19" rectangle. Slide a decorative arch piece (E) between the stops and bend it around the curve (see photo, top right).
2. Place two hoops between the top and middle crossbars aligned with the legs and the 10" mark. Mark where the legs cross the middle crossbar, cut and weld in place.
3. Place a hoop with one leg at the 5" mark and the other at the 15" mark. Mark, cut, and weld (see photo, middle right).
4. Cut a hoop in half and place the halves starting from the 5" and 15" weld in place.
5. Repeat Steps 2 to 4 for the other side panel.

FINISH THE ARCHES

1. Remove the quarter circles from the bending jig. From the right angles of the quarter circles, measure in 7½" along one flat side. At this point, draw a line perpendicular to the side (see photo, bottom right). Cut along the line. Repeat with the second quarter circle.
2. Mount these two arcs at the top of a 4 × 8 sheet of plywood, abutting them together on the new cuts to create a template for the arches. Place stop blocks 1" from the arc.
3. Place one arch into the left side of the jig. Mark a vertical line on the arch to match the joint of the two wood arcs. Cut the arch along the line. (See bottom left photo, page 97.)
4. Place the other arch into the right side of the jig. Mark the centreline and cut.
5. Place both arches back into the jig and weld together at the peak. Repeat Steps 3 and 4 for the second arch. Remove the arch jig from the plywood sheet.

ASSEMBLE THE ARCHWAY

1. Cut the sleeves (F) to length. Cut the arch crossbars (G) to length.
2. Mark two parallel lines 45" apart on the sides of the plywood. Attach 2 × 4 clamping blocks along these lines.
3. Clamp the two side panels, lying on their backs, to the jig.
4. Slide sleeves into the legs 1", and weld in place.

Make a bending jig to create the hoops for the decorative arches.

Align the top of the hoop with the top crossbar and mark where the legs cross the middle crossbar.

After bending the main arches, remove the quarter circles from the jig. Mark in 7½" from one flat edge and cut the form down.

5. Slide an arch over the sleeves and weld in place (see photo, page 102). Repeat with the second arch.
6. Weld a crossbar (G) between the two arches at the peak. Weld crossbars spaced 9" apart on the sides of the arches (see top photo, opposite page).

MAKE THE GATE FRAME

1. Cut the gate uprights (H) and crossbars (I) to length.
2. Lay out the two gate frames with the crossbars on the top and bottom of the uprights. Place the third crossbar 10" from the top of the uprights. Check for square and tack-weld together. Check the diagonals and adjust if necessary. Finish the welds.
3. Cut the gate verticals (J) to length. Mark all three crossbars at $5\frac{3}{16}$", $10\frac{3}{16}$", and $15\frac{3}{16}$". Center the verticals at the marks. Check for square and weld in place (see centre photo, opposite page).
4. Make and assemble the gate decorative arches using the same method as described under Create the Decorative Arches.

INSTALL THE GATE

1. Stand the archway upright. Using scrap metal or wood, clamp the archway legs so that the space between the legs is 45" and the panels are parallel.
2. Align the gates flush with a set of legs (the legs and gate are flush front to back) and clamp in place. Allow a slight gap between the gates and legs (the gap is between the legs and gate side to side).
3. Tack-weld the hinges (K) in place (see bottom photo, opposite page). Remove the clamps holding the gates and check that the gates swing freely. Adjust if necessary and complete the welds. Install the gate latch (L).

FINISH THE ARCHWAY

1. If you plan to finish the archway, sand or wire brush or sandblast it. Apply the finish of your choice.
2. Install the archway by clamping the side panels 45" apart.
3. On the ground where the arch will be installed, mark a 21 × 46" rectangle. At the corners of the rectangle, pound the mounting stakes 1 foot into the ground. Lift the archway onto the mounting stakes and remove the clamps.

Clamp the sides to clamping blocks on a 4 × 8 sheet of plywood. Slide the main arches over the angle iron sleeves in the legs.

Weld the arch crossbars to the arches.

Centre the gate verticals at the marks and weld in place.

Use shims and clamps to hold the gates in place. Weld the base, pin side of the hinge to the frame and the top to the gate.

Gazebo

This moderate-size gazebo is also a special addition to any yard. Big enough for a table and chairs, it is small enough to fit in all but the tiniest of yards. Covered with vines in the summer, it provides delightful shade. In the off-season it supplies a point of visual interest with its scrolling patterns.

The directions here describe how to build door, window, and roof panels. The material quantities are for a gazebo with three door panels and three window panels. You can choose to construct your gazebo with any combinations, just remember to accordingly adjust your quantities list.

MATERIALS

- 4" finial (1, Decorative Iron #126)
- 1 × 1" square tube (344 feet)
- 3/16" round rod (1,000 feet)
- 1/2" round tube (6 feet)
- 3/8" round rod (10 1/2 feet)
- 1/4" round rod (3 feet)
- 4 1/2" drip trays (2)
- 2" round tube (2")
- 1/2 × 6" carriage bolt, nut, and washer (1)
- 3/4" round rod or rebar (9 feet)

Finial detail

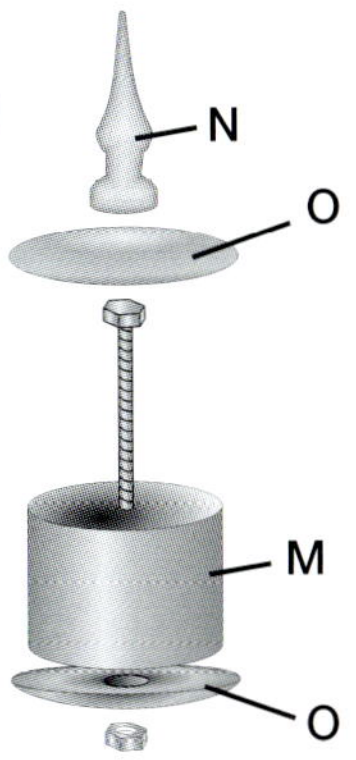

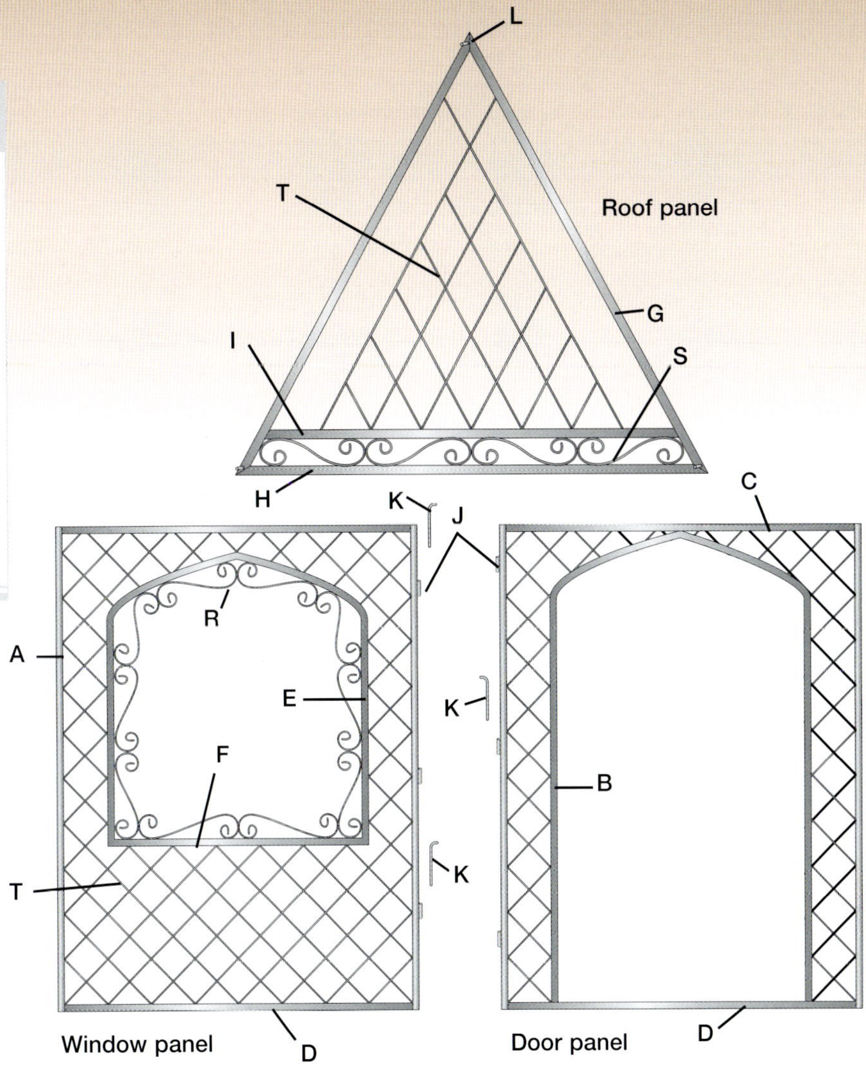

PART	NAME	DIMENSIONS	QUANTITY
A	Legs	16-gauge 1 × 1" square tube × 80"	12
B	Door frames	16-gauge 1 × 1" square tube × 96"	6
C	Top crossbars	16-gauge 1 × 1" square tube × 54"	6
D	Bottom crossbars	16-gauge 1 × 1" square tube × 52"	6
E	Window frames	16-gauge 1 × 1" square tube × 40"	6
F	Window crossbars	16-gauge 1 × 1" square tube × 30"*	6
G	Roof sides	16-gauge 1 × 1" square tube × 66 1/2"	12
H	Roof bases	16-gauge 1 × 1" square tube × 61"	6
I	Roof crossbars	16-gauge 1 × 1" square tube × 61"*	6
J	Hinge barrels	16-gauge 1/2" round tube × 3"	24
K	Hinge pins	3/8" round rod × 7 1/2"	12
L	Finial pegs	1/4" round rod × 6"	6
M	Finial sleeve	16-gauge 2" round tube × 2"	1
N	Finial	4"	1
O	Drip trays	4 1/2"	2
P	Roof pegs	3/8" round rod × 3"	12
Q	Peg sleeves	16-gauge 1/2" round tube × 3"	12
R	Window scrolls	3/16" round rod × 24"	30
S	Roof scrolls	3/16" round rod × 36"	24
T	Diagonals	3/16" round rod × varied*	624

* Cut to fit.

How to Build a Gazebo

Before welding, thoroughly clean all parts with denatured alcohol.

Make the Door Panels

1. Cut two legs (A), two door frames (B), a top crossbar (C), and bottom crossbar (D) to length. Mitre one end of each leg at 45°, and both ends of the top crossbar at 45°.
2. Lay out the legs, top crossbar, and bottom crossbar to form a rectangle. The bottom crossbar fits between the legs.
3. Check the rectangle for square and tack-weld all corners.
4. Mark the door frames at 24". Using a conduit bender, bend the frames at the mark to 50° (see photo, below).
5. Place the door frames inside the assembled panel frame. Align the door frames 8" in from the panel sides. Mark vertical lines on the door frames where they overlap at the peak. Cut on the marks and tack-weld the door frame arch together.
6. Align the door frame arch inside the panel frame with the point of the arch touching the top crossbar. Mark the legs where they cross the bottom crossbar. Cut the legs to length. Tack-weld the door frame to the top and bottom crossbars.
7. Repeat steps 1 through 6 to make the desired number of door panels. Complete the welds.

Make the Window Panels

1. Cut two window frames (E) and a window crossbar (F) to length.
2. Mark the window frames at 24". Using a conduit bender, bend the frames at the mark to 50° (see photo).
3. Lay out the window frames with the window crossbar between two legs (A). Mark the vertical line at the peak where the frames cross each other. Cut the frames on the line and tack-weld together.
4. Trim the legs to length, if necessary. Tack-weld the window crossbar in place. Put the window frame aside for later installation.
5. Repeat Steps 1 through 4 to make the desired number of window panels.

Make the Roof Panels

1. Cut two roof sides (G) to length. Mitre one end of each side at 29°. Align the mitred edges and tack-weld.
2. Cut a roof base (H) to size. Evenly align it underneath the sides. Mark where the sides cross the base. Cut on this line. Tack-weld the base to the sides.
3. Cut a roof crossbar (I) to size. Place the crossbar 5" up from the roof base and mark the angles where the roof sides cross the crossbar (see top photo, opposite page).
4. Repeat Steps 1 to 3 to make the remaining five roof panels. Complete the welds.

Assemble the Gazebo

Assembling the gazebo before all the decorations are added makes it lighter and easier to maneuver. In addition, if a panel is slightly skewed, it is easier to make corrections without having to rearrange decorative elements. Because the hinges will be perfectly aligned only for one arrangement, make sure you assemble the panels in the order desired.

1. Cut the hinge barrels (J) and pins (K) to length. With a bench vise, bend a right angle ½" in from one end of each pin.
2. Slide a pin into two barrels. Place two panels on the floor or upright against a wall. Place the barrels against the joint between the panels at 20" from the top. Tack-weld one barrel to one panel and the other barrel to the second panel (see bottom photo, opposite page).
3. Tack-weld another hinge to the panels at about 20" from the bottom.

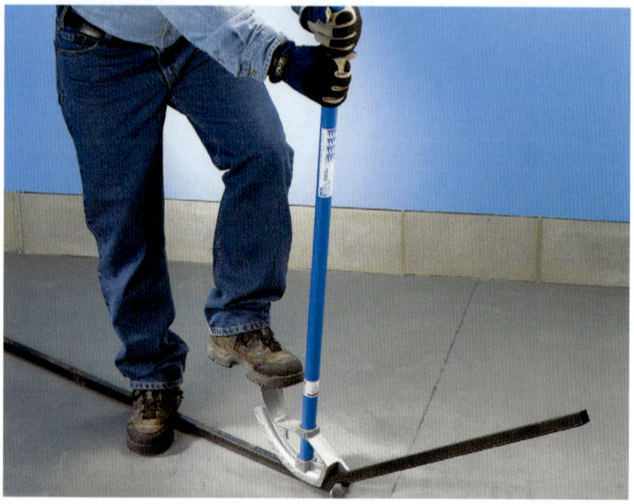

Create the window and door arches by bending the tubing with a large conduit bender.

4. Repeat Steps 2 and 3 with the two other sets of two panels.
5. With the panels standing, arrange the three sets of two panels to form a hexagon. The angle between each panel pair should be 120°.
6. Install hinges at the remaining three panel joints.

ASSEMBLE THE FINIAL

1. Cut the finial pegs (L) to length. Bend the finial pegs in half to 110°. Support the roof sections on a cinder block or stool and tack-weld a finial peg to the point of each roof section (see photo, top left on page 108).
2. Cut the finial sleeve (M) to length.
3. Weld the finial (N) to the centre of one drip tray (O) on the convex side.
4. Grind down the head of a ½ × 6" carriage bolt until it matches the concave curve of the drip tray. Welt the carriage bolt to the middle of the concave side of the drip tray from Step 3 (see top right photo, page 108).
5. Center the finial sleeve over the bolt and weld in place. Drill a 9⁄16" hole through the centre of the second drip tray.
6. With the peaks of the roof panels resting on a cinder block or low stool, slide the finial assembly over the finial pegs. Bend the finial pegs if necessary to fit inside the finial sleeve.

ASSEMBLE THE ROOF

Assembling the roof is easiest with an assistant or two.

1. Cut the roof pegs (P) and peg sleeves (Q) to length.
2. Weld two sleeves to the tops of each side panel, ¾" in from the sides of the legs (see photo, top left on page 109).
3. Measure the distance between a pair of sleeves. Use this measurement to mark the peg locations on a roof panel. Grind the pegs to 60° on one end and weld the ground end to the roof panel.
4. With the side panels assembled, place a roof section on top of a wall panel, sliding the pegs into the sleeves. Have an assistant hold up the centre of the roof, or create a wood support.
5. Place the remaining roof sections. Slide the finial over the finial pegs, slide the drip cup over the bolt, and install the washer and nut.
6. Adjust roof and finial pegs as needed.

Mark the roof crossbar for cutting.

Insert a hinge pin into two hinge barrels. Place the hinge between two side panels and weld one barrel to one panel and the other barrel to the adjoining panel.

Support roof sections on a cinder block. Weld the finial pegs to the points of the panels.

Create the finial assembly by welding the finial to the drip tray, then welding the bolt to the drip tray.

7. Number or otherwise mark the side and roof panels for reassembly.
8. Remove the finial and take the roof panels down. Disassemble the panels by pounding out the hinge pins.

MAKE THE WINDOW SCROLLS

1. Cut the scroll blanks (R) to length.
2. Cut a 3⁄16" slot in a 2" pipe. Place the rod in both slots, then bend the rod around the outside of the pipe 1½ times (see right photo, opposite page).
3. Place the other end of the rod in the slot and bend 1½ turns around the outside of the pipe in the opposite direction.
4. Slightly open the bends to create a pleasing scroll.
5. Repeat to form the remaining window scrolls.
6. Weld the scrolls into the window frames as pictured.

MAKE THE ROOF SCROLLS

1. Cut the scroll blanks (S) to length.
2. Cut a 3⁄16" in a 3" pipe. Place the rod through both slots, then bend the rod around the outside of the pipe 1½ times.
3. Place the other end of the rod in the slot and bend 1½ turns around the outside of the pipe in the opposite direction.
4. Slightly open or close the bends to make the scroll fit between the roof base and roof crossbar.
5. Repeat for the other roof scrolls.
6. Weld the scrolls between the roof base and roof crossbar as pictured.

ADD DECORATION TO THE ROOF

You can make the roof a simple diamond pattern.

1. To make the diagonals (T), mark the roof sides every 6" down from the peak and 6" down from the roof crossbar. Lay out two rods from the peak marks to the opposite first two marks on the roof crossbar to match the roof panel diagram (page 105). Cut the rods to fit and weld in place.
2. Mark the diagonals from Step 1 every 6".
3. Make the internal diagonals by cutting pieces to fit between the marks on the right side and base. Weld in place.
4. Finish the internal diagonals by cutting pieces to fit between the marks on the left side and base. Weld in place.

Weld the roof sleeves to the tops of the side panels.

Cut a 3⁄16" notch in a 2" pipe to create the bending jig for the scrolls. Slide the rod into the notch, then bend the rod around the pipe.

ADD DIAGONAL FILLER TO SIDE PANELS

Diagonal rods can fill the space below and above the windows, or you can add scrolls and hearts.

1. On the door panels, mark the legs, door frames, and top crossbars every 8".
2. Cut diagonals to fit between the marks.
3. Weld the descending left to right diagonals in place, then weld the ascending left to right diagonals in place.
4. On the window panels, mark the legs, top and bottom crossbars, window frames, and window crossbars every 8". Align the window frame between the legs, 8" in from each side with the 8" marks aligned. The bottom of the window should be 32" from the bottom crossbar.
5. Cut diagonals to fit between the marks on the window frame and legs.
6. Cut diagonals to fit between the marks on the crossbars and the window frames and window crossbars.
7. Weld the descending left to right diagonals in place, then weld the ascending left to right diagonals in place.

FINISH THE GAZEBO

1. Wire brush or sand blast the gazebo. Finish as desired. Note: Take care to track the panel numbers so you can reassemble the gazebo.
2. Reassemble the gazebo.
3. For at least three corners of the gazebo, pound 3-foot lengths of 3⁄4" round bar or 18" rebar into the ground and slide the leg ends over the bars.

METRICS

Converting Measurements

To Convert:	To:	Multiply by:
Inches	Millimeters	25.4
Inches	Centimeters	2.54
Feet	Meters	0.305
Yards	Meters	0.914
Square inches	Square centimeters	6.45
Square feet	Square meters	0.093
Square yards	Square meters	0.836
Cubic inches	Cubic centimeters	16.4
Cubic feet	Cubic meters	0.0283
Cubic yards	Cubic meters	0.765
Ounces	Millileters	30.0
Pints (U.S.)	Liters	0.473 (Imp. 0.568)
Quarts (U.S.)	Liters	0.946 (Imp. 1.136)
Gallons (U.S.)	Liters	3.785 (Imp. 4.546)
Ounces	Grams	28.4
Pounds	Kilograms	0.454

To Convert:	To:	Multiply by:
Millimeters	Inches	0.039
Centimeters	Inches	0.394
Meters	Feet	3.28
Meters	Yards	1.09
Square centimeters	Square inches	0.155
Square meters	Square feet	10.8
Square meters	Square yards	1.2
Cubic centimeters	Cubic inches	0.061
Cubic meters	Cubic feet	35.3
Cubic meters	Cubic yards	1.31
Millileters	Ounces	.033
Liters	Pints (U.S.)	2.114 (Imp. 1.76)
Liters	Quarts (U.S.)	1.057 (Imp. 0.88)
Liters	Gallons (U.S.)	0.264 (Imp. 0.22)
Grams	Ounces	0.035
Kilograms	Pounds	2.2

Sheet Metal Thickness

Gauge	Inch	mm
0	0.0157	0.3988
28	0.0187	0.4750
26	0.0217	0.5512
24	0.0276	0.7010
22	0.0336	0.8534
20	0.0396	1.0058
18	0.0516	1.3106
16	0.0635	1.6129
14	0.0785	1.9939
12	0.1084	2.7534
10	0.1382	3.5103
8	0.1681	4.2697

INDEX